Together

Together

Stories and Poems by

Julius Chingono

&

John Eppel

'amaBooks

Published in Europe and Africa by 'amaBooks
P.O. Box AC1066
Ascot, Bulawayo
Zimbabwe
www.amabooksbyo.com
ISBN: 978-0-7974-4228-3 ('amaBooks)

Published in South Africa by University of KwaZulu-Natal Press
Private Bag X01
Scottsville, 3209
South Africa
Email: books@ukzn.ac.za
www.ukznpress.co.za
ISBN: 978-1-86914-213-1 (University of KwaZulu-Natal Press)

Published in North America by UNO Press; distributed by
   National Book Network
ISBN: 978-1-60801-049-3 (UNO Press)
Library of Congress Control Number: 2011920592

© Collection: 'amaBooks, 2011
© Individual contributions: the authors

No part of this publication may be reproduced, stored in a retrieval system, or transmitted in any form or by any means, electronic, mechanical, photocopying, recording or otherwise, without the prior permission of the publisher.

This book is a work of fiction: any characters, organisations and situations mentioned bear no relation to any real person, organisation or actual happening.

Cover painting by Marshall Baron, from the collection of Lene Lauritsen
Photographs of John Eppel and Julius Chingono courtesy of Andre F.
   van Rooyen and Julius Chingono
Book and cover design by Carrie Chappell

Contents

Acknowledgements	ix
About the Authors	x
Introduction	xii
JULIUS CHINGONO	1
Curiosity	3
My False Tooth	4
Leave My Bible Alone	5
A Caged Lion	9
Doves	10
We Waited	11
20-044L	24
No Funeral	25
A Buzz	26
Shonongoro	27
A Demon	29
Pregnant	30
A Portrait	31
The Dread Gentleman	32
At the Bus Station	40
Candy Mercenaries	41
Second Look	42
The Toilet Issue	43

Drunk	48
This is Harassment	49
Slogans	50
The Score	51
I Lost a Verse	53
Greetings	54
Tired Feet	55
Our Boss	56
Doubt	61
Shortages	62
Wrong	63
Murehwa	64
Why My Love	72
You Know What I Mean	73
JOHN EPPEL	75
Malnourished Sonnet	77
Afrika	78
The Debate	79
The Coming of the Rains	83
Ghostly Galleon	84
Democracy at Work and at Play	86
Day and Night	92
The CWM	93
Broke-Buttock Blues	96
Discarded	97
Song for WOZA	100
Soap Rhymes With Hope	101
The Big Five	102
Sick at Heart	105
Charles Dickens Visits Bulawayo	106
Who Will Guard the Guards?	108

The Cage	110
Sapphics to our Redeemer	111
Two Metres of Drainage Pipe	112
Haiku with One Extra Syllable	114
Rearranged Haiku	115
Empties	116
Bhalagwe Blues	118
Shards	119
Boys will be Boys	120
Via Dolorosa	123
He Shakes More Than He Can Hold	124
The Floating Straw Hat	125
English Sonnet in Broken Metre	129
The Honourable Minister Speaks	130
The Pact	132
Yet Another Flower Poem	143
Emperor Moth	144
Bloody Diamonds	145
Culture	148
Waiting	149
Glossary	151

Acknowledgements

The publishers and the writers would like to thank the Zimbabwe Culture Fund Trust for their support for this project, Tinashe Muchuri and Togara Muzanenhamo for their assistance with Julius Chingono's work and Dr Drew Shaw for the introduction.

Extracts: *The song of a child who survived Nyadzonia*, Emmanuel Ngara, in *Songs from the Temple*, Mambo Press, 1992; *Alice Blue Gown*, Joseph McCarthy, 1919.

Doves and *The Coming of the Rains* were first published on www.zimbabwe.poetryinternational.org; *My False Tooth* and *I Lost a Verse* on medusaskitchen.blogspot.com; *20-044L*, *Discarded*, *The Honourable Minister Speaks* and *The Floating Straw Hat* in *The Warwick Review*, United Kingdom; *Via Dolorosa* in *New Contrast*, South Africa; *Broke-Buttock Blues*, *Bloody Diamonds* and *Yet Another Flower Poem* in *Quadrant*, Australia; *Song for WOZA* and *Sick at Heart* in *Illuminations*, USA; *Soap Rhymes With Hope* and *Bhalagwe Blues* in *New Coin*, South Africa; *Who Will Guard the Guards* in *Critical Arts*, South Africa (www.informaworld.com); *Haiku with One Extra Syllable*, *Rearranged Haiku*, *Boys will be Boys*, *The CWM*, *Two Metres of Drainage Pipe* and *Ghostly Galleon* on www.kubatana.net; *Day and Night* and *Culture* in *Carapace*, South Africa; *Shards* and *Waiting* in *Intwasa Poetry*, 'amaBooks, 2008; *English Sonnet in Broken Metre* in www.pambazuka.org.

Julius Chingono

Born in 1946 on a commercial farm near Harare, Julius Chingono spent most of his working life as a rock blaster in the mines. He wrote in both Shona and English, and won awards for poems written in both languages.

He had five books published: one play, *Ruvimbo*; one novel, *Chipo Changu*; two poetry collections, *Flag of Rags* and *Kazwi*; and one collection of short stories and poetry, *Not Another Day*.

His poem *They are picked* was chosen by *New Internationalist* for their collection *Fire in the Soul*, of the best 100 human rights poems from across the world over the last 100 years.

Julius read his poetry at various international festivals, including the Poetry International Festival in the Netherlands, Poetry Africa in Durban, and the Shaari International Poetry Festival in Israel.

He died in January 2011, after a short illness.

John Eppel

Born in South Africa in 1947, John Eppel was raised in Zimbabwe, where he still lives, teaching English at Christian Brothers College in Bulawayo. His first novel, *D G G Berry's The Great North Road*, won the M-Net prize and was listed in the *Weekly Mail & Guardian* as one of the best 20 South African books in English published between 1948 and 1994. His second novel, *Hatchings*, was shortlisted for the M-Net prize and was chosen for the series in the *Times Literary Supplement* of the most significant books to have come out of Africa. His other novels are *The Giraffe Man*, *The Curse of the Ripe Tomato*, *The Holy Innocents* and *Absent: The English Teacher*.

His poetry collections include *Spoils of War*, which won the Ingrid Jonker Prize, *Sonata for Matabeleland*, *Selected Poems: 1965–1995* and *Songs My Country Taught Me*. He has written two collections of poetry and short stories: *The Caruso of Colleen Bawn* and *White Man Crawling*.

John's short stories and poems have appeared in many anthologies, journals and websites, including six poems in the *Penguin Anthology of South African Poetry*. His poem *Vendor and Child* was chosen by *New Internationalist* for their collection *Fire in the Soul*, of the best 100 human rights poems from across the world over the last 100 years.

Introduction

Julius Chingono and John Eppel became friends when they met at the Intwasa Arts Festival in Bulawayo in 2007. 'amaBooks Publishers and the two writers discerned a creative link, a joint-publication was proposed, and the result is this collaboration. The various pieces gathered here are fictional or poetic reflections on post-independence Zimbabwe. In a country that has been beset with destructive divisions, it is refreshing to witness an initiative to unite two writers of different social backgrounds, cultures and perspectives, in a project symbolically titled *Together*. The title implies a unity, a solidarity of sorts, and the links, we discover, are many.

    I first met the authors at the Harare International Festival of the Arts (HIFA) in May 2009, where I noticed an instant rapport. John Eppel had emerged from a heated round table discussion about the challenges facing the artist during national crisis, where he had praised the commitment of writers, especially those remaining in Zimbabwe. The mood lightened as soon as Julius met John at the Poetry Café to have a drink. I asked Julius, in December 2010, what connected him to John and he said he believed it was "humour and realism". Of Julius, John said, "I found him to be a warm-hearted man with a mind like a razor-blade." Julius, from the small town of Norton near Harare, was a rock-blaster in mines for many years. John, from Bulawayo, teaches English literature (but his father, he told me, was also a rock-blaster).

    In a literary sense, the authors seem an 'odd couple'. Eppel is a self-conscious stylist, steeped in the Western literary tradition (in which he continuously situates himself – albeit with much irony). By contrast, Chingono is an anti-stylist, who does not follow any literary mentors, he told me, and does not consciously write within any recognisable tradition. Yet Eppel read and commended Chingono's poetry, recognising him immediately as "a poet of transcendence". Chingono likewise appreciated Eppel's poetry and, during a talk at the National Gallery of Zimbabwe in Bulawayo, praised the satire in Eppel's writing, which a few had misconstrued as racist. Together, they developed a close professional and personal bond, and could be seen at festivals drinking and laughing, while commenting – as most Zimbabweans are in the habit of doing – on the state of the nation.

Both could play the Fool, yet earned reputations as 'clever clowns'. The Fool in Western literature is a witty figure credited with speaking a truth that others cannot. The Griot – a similar figure in West African literary and cultural tradition – grasps local history impressively and his wit can be devastating. Qualities of the Fool or the Griot can be found in both Eppel and Chingono, though both hail from southern Africa and did not necessarily cultivate this reputation consciously.

Other similarities are many: both were born in the mid-1940s, within a year of each other, and began writing in the 1960s. Both are accomplished prose-writers yet consider themselves poets primarily; both speak out against poverty and social injustice, yet also infuse their writing with wry humour. Julius Chingono's work is in Shona and English; John Eppel writes only in English, though he sometimes incorporates Ndebele vocabulary.

Of their differences, Julius told me, "He is white and I am black, but we are all Zimbabwean . . . I believe in people living together in harmony. Fighting poverty being our main agenda." John Eppel likewise believes in multiculturalism, but views the fight against poverty more radically: "I disagree with Jesus that the poor will always be with us," he told me. "Poverty, unlike religion or vulgar capitalism, is a virus that will be eradicated, as it almost has been in a few countries. What angers me is that it is taking so long. And it is because of the shocking greed of people in power, corporate as well as political." Greed and power, an elite class of 'chefs' (bosses) trampling on a disempowered, impoverished 'povo' (ordinary people) are themes that recur in the stories and poems of both authors.

The setting for most pieces is the post-2000 period, a decade of unprecedented decline and hardship in Zimbabwe.[1] This began with white farmers' land being expropriated in the 'Fast Track' redistribution exercise, eventually displacing around 900 000 farm workers and dependents. The elections of 2000 sparked clashes between supporters of Robert Mugabe's ZANU-PF, in power since independence in 1980, and the newly-formed opposition Movement for Democratic Change (MDC). Unemployment, inflation and emigration soared and the economy went into tailspin. 2005 brought new elections and more clashes, then the bulldozing of informal settlements in Operation Murambatsvina (translated as 'clear out the filth'), when another 700 000 people were displaced and lost their livelihoods. By 2006, 85 per cent of Zimbabweans were living below the poverty line, according to a United Nations report. Throughout the decade an AIDS pandemic also raged; and life expectancy dropped to the lowest in the world, thirty-seven for men and thirty-four for women – largely because of a breakdown in healthcare services. 2008 saw more disputed elections, violence, hyper-inflation, chronic food shortages, and a cholera outbreak – all of which brought the country to its knees. Opposing political parties eventually negotiated a Government of National Unity (GNU) and 2009 brought some economic stabilization with the scrapping of the Zimbabwean dollar and US currency 'dollarization'. 2010 saw tensions in power-sharing but also nation-wide canvassing of public opinion on a new constitution.

The above events form the backdrop of the stories and poems in *Together*, which mostly tell the tale of a troubled nation and people struggling within it. Additionally, John Eppel returns in time to the 1980s, when the North Korean-trained Fifth Brigade brutally quelled dissent in Matabeleland, then a stronghold of Joshua Nkomo's opposing ZAPU (Zimbabwe African People's Union), in Operation Gukurahundi (translated as 'the rain that sweeps away the chaff'). By 1997, the Catholic Commission for Justice and Peace (CCJP) had published *Breaking the Silence*, a detailed report on the atrocities, which showed the violence was

---

1. Brian Raftopoulos, *The Crisis in Zimbabwe*, in *Becoming Zimbabwe* (Harare, Weaver Press, 2009)

ethnically-based, with the minority Ndebele in rural areas being targeted as perceived enemies of the Zimbabwean state. But there was never a Truth and Reconciliation Commission to begin a process of national healing. An art exhibition on the subject was banned at the National Art Gallery in Bulawayo in 2010; and the artist, Owen Maseko, now faces a prison sentence if convicted of charges brought against him.

Strikingly, in this collection, both authors offer a heightened awareness of class issues, which have long been eclipsed by nationalist sentiments in politics and the official media. The poems and stories, as they are arranged, talk to each other on inter-related issues, offering the reader a varied reading experience, yet also some thematic unity.

Julius Chingono's work catches the everyday hardships of the working class, trying to survive demeaning conditions. The sign on the speaker's door in the poem *20-044L* is an old number plate in a scrap metal collage, signifying creative ingenuity regardless of one's material conditions. Nevertheless, the author is highly critical of a failed socialist revolution, where the poor remain oppressed; and he exposes a dehumanizing system where only a newly-privileged elite are reaping benefits. "They knew that government was a soulless machine that did not have blood flowing through its veins," states the narrator in *The Dread Gentleman*, where a Murambatsvina survivor somehow rises above the devastation. Corruption is rife: *Our Boss*, set on a 'new farm', follows a well-connected beneficiary of Fast Track land reform, a boss who "uses his right boot to send his instructions home" and gets his workers to dump donated fertilizer into a dam to remove evidence of its theft.

Zimbabwe is drawn as a starkly stratified society of 'haves' and 'have nots' and Julius Chingono rejects the repeated ideology of consumerism: *This is Harassment* is a poem protesting against billboards and relentless advertising – bombarding even those who can never afford what is on offer. A warped capitalistic value system is also challenged in *I Lost a Verse* where a businessman interrupts the writer for his pen so as not to lose an order – not considering that the poet thereby loses a verse. Why, we are asked, is the businessman's work automatically presumed more important in this society?

But it is the exploited as well as the exploiters that Julius Chingono takes to task. Observing a tendency for the poor to turn against each other, his writing highlights their failure to identify the real sources of oppression and unite against them. An example is *The Toilet Issue*, a farcical anecdote about male and female lodgers embarrassing each other in an ill-designed, overworked communal outhouse – leading to angry exchanges, bruises and even broken teeth. The exploitative landlord, meanwhile, cares only about damage to his property.

The exploited have lost their dignity, and Chingono draws fractured communities where self-survival is now the norm. In the poem *At the Bus Station*, the speaker is jostled and squashed in a demoralizing competition by commuters to scramble onto an overloaded bus. Conflict amongst the working class is also evident at a football match, where a disputed goal nearly results in all-out battle between rival fans in *The Score*. In the poem *Greetings* even the most basic of human communications are now emptied of meaning.

What can be done by the people, 'the povo', to halt this downward spiral, to take charge of their fate? In *We Waited* we get an answer, yet the story is depressing. Grassroots voters try to regain control of the party representing them, but their candidates are disqualified by trumped-up technicalities. When they protest against corruption, they are tragically mowed down in a suspicious 'accident', which bleakly ends their promising initiative.

But the tenor in this collection is not all doom and gloom. Chingono also makes mirth of the subject of death as we see in the dark comedy *Murehwa*, about a bachelor who dies with an erection, considered a bad omen in his village. Women are brought in to ritually dance around the corpse, secretly wearing no underwear, so as to 'relieve' the dead man before his final burial.

Although we are made to laugh at death, the author's lighthearted attitude did not prepare many for his own sudden departure. After a short illness, Julius Chingono died on 2nd January 2011; and two of his poems portend his own fate uncannily. In *A Demon* the deceased is cursed for dying at the most joyous time of the year "to douse the festive season/ with sobbing handkerchiefs" while *No Funeral* pleads for "no ceremony, no speeches, no coffin" in the event of death because the speaker would rather disappear without trace. But it is unlikely Julius Chingono will be able to simply vanish – at least from his important place in Zimbabwean literature. He moreover earned international recognition when he attended the Poetry International Festival in Rotterdam in 2004, which was the first time he had ever left Zimbabwe.

With many of his poems he reflects philosophically on broader human concerns – birth, death, children, marriage, divorce, and the process of aging. He is a man of few words – but wise ones that are carefully chosen. "Art does not thrive/ on half truths/ like politics..." says the speaker in *A Buzz*. This neatly summarizes the appeal of his own poetry, which, despite its apparent simplicity, provokes deep considerations of the 'whole truth'. The poems are charged with proverbial wisdom, yet they also convey the thoughts and feelings of an individual with a distinctive style of his own. This collection comprises his latest and last writings.

Turning to the work of the other author in this partnership: John Eppel also shows that the struggle in Zimbabwe is primarily about class. If Chingono succeeds especially in conveying working class concerns, Eppel is most effective at satirizing the bourgeois and ruling classes.

Seizing the means of production is meant to empower the masses, Eppel observes, not just an elite few; and merely changing the complexion of capitalism amounts to a betrayal of Zimbabwe's original socialist ideals. His satires are therefore mercilessly critical of the new 'chefs', their greed, and abuse of power.

Boys Will be Boys caricatures the 'Boys Club' that is pervasive in politics, regardless it seems of the party. PAPA and DADDY (ridiculed with absurd acronyms) are locked in negotiations to establish powersharing, but more concerned about the five-star-hotel trappings, the drinks and the perks that come with the job.

Greed and corruption are treated more seriously in other pieces. *Bloody Diamonds*, for example, documents the diamond rush in Chiadzwa, now judged one of the largest diamond fields in the world, a heavily militarized zone where many have perished. The protagonist in this case is killed by helicopter fire as he fills his bag with precious stones. Zimbabwe's newfound mineral wealth lines the pockets of a corrupt few but is a curse rather than a blessing for the poor, it seems.

Nevertheless, there is a glimmer of hope that the poor – particularly the youth – have become resourceful, and this will equip them for the challenges ahead. *Empties* is a sketch about a struggling twelve-year-old, who finds empty bottles worth much more than what he is paid to clean out a suburban garage.

Bulawayo's suburbs are once again the setting for satire, as John Eppel turns his sights on the aging white community. In *The CWM* (Cheeky White Madam), Mrs MacSnatch, with her blue-rinsed hair and crease-resistant clothes, puts a stop to cock-crowing, neglected "pussies", boisterous "bow-wows", "brats" and loud music as she neatens the neighbourhood she invades. Comic satire turns darker, however, in *The Pact*, where four widowed white women – struggling to survive Zimbabwe's meltdown – decide that if life gets too burdensome for one, all will commit suicide together. When their charity soup kitchen is hijacked by violent youths declaring, "You whites are thieves. That soup comes from the land, which you stole from our people", the well-meaning women come face to face with the unstoppable assault of ethnic nationalism, which seems to have garnered a life form of its own.

The violence surrounding elections in 2008 is a theme in several poems, where John Eppel uses a public voice to sound praises and to voice protest. *Broke-Buttock Blues* draws on the rhythm of the blues, originally developed by African-American slaves, to mournfully register the pain of oppression and to challenge it. *Song for WOZA* is a heroic praise poem dedicated to Women of Zimbabwe Arise – activists in the forefront of human rights campaigning. *The Ghostly Galleon* is another example of comrades formally praised for their bravery: this time the speaker celebrates the solidarity of the Durban dockers who stopped a Chinese ship from off-loading her deadly cargo of weaponry destined for Zimbabwe.

There are no loyalties in politics ultimately, Eppel suggests in *Discarded*, where Willibald Nyoni, a war veteran deployed "to intimidate rural folk into voting 'wisely'" steals an ox "as part of the continuing struggle" – only to be arrested after the poll for stock theft, then sent to jail for nine years. In another satire, *Democracy at Work and Play*, a well-meaning team of outreach workers are unceremoniously forced to leave Kezi by angry war veterans but not before facing a barrage of controversial opinions such as "homosexuals should be stoned to death in public," "girls should not be raped before they are 24 years old," and "we should have a president for life." It will be a rocky road to the attainment of a new democratic constitution in Zimbabwe, the outreach team discovers.

As part of his ambitious project to document all of Zimbabwe's troubled recent history, and believing that 'breaking the silence' can lead to national healing, John Eppel addresses the taboo subject of Gukurahundi. Drawing on testimonies from actual survivors, Eppel seeks through fiction to identify with the victims – to commemorate them as thinking, feeling people rather than mere casualties who have now become statistics. In *Two Metres of Drainage Pipe*, the narrator shouts at children playing in a disused drainage pipe because it triggers traumatic memories of how her brother was tortured to death inside two metres of drainage pipe. Bhalagwe was a notorious torture and death camp. *Bhalagwe Blues* and *Shards* address the horrors of Gukurahundi in poetic form.

John Eppel's poetry is meticulously crafted, and presented in a variety of forms, such as the blues, praise poetry, satiric poetry, narrative poetry, sonnets, sestinas, and even the Japanese haiku. Here it is more experimental than usual in its effort to chronicle historic moments for posterity, to address difficult subjects, to identify with and express solidarity with struggling people. The reader will judge the degree to which Eppel succeeds with each poem. Notwithstanding, his effort to break new ground, to find appropriate poetic expression for these realities, is brave and highly commendable.

Both Chingono and Eppel comment on local history in some detail and with a sharp wit that is often devastating. In exposing systems of inequality and injustice they moreover displace the grand narrative of nationalism, supplanting it with that of class consciousness. With both authors there is disillusionment with a post-independence dispensation yet some hope that the impoverished may eventually triumph. Never far from the hardships of 'the povo', and with his 'razor-blade' perception, Chingono communicates proletarian realities especially well. Eppel's forte, on the other hand, is satirizing the newly empowered middle class and exposing the self-serving interests of a corrupt ruling elite. Together, in their 'double act', these 'clever clowns' have a large arsenal of highly creative critical commentary and are a formidable pair.

Drew Shaw, Midlands State University, Zimbabwe

JULIUS CHINGONO

Curiosity

He heard sounds
of guns firing outside
in the streets.
He opened the door
slightly to see,
but he never saw
the bullet
that killed his curiosity.

My False Tooth

A false tooth
got lost
in a tongue dance
that was full of froth
and mist,
it was found later
holding onto a gum.

Leave My Bible Alone

Every Sunday morning Mudhara Gore attended the service at his parish church, St Barnabas. His wife, MaMoyo, woke up very early to fetch water from the communal bathrooms; this water she heated on a wood-stove outside the house. Soon afterwards Gore joined her to get ready to leave for the service, which started at 9 o'clock. Bathing. Breakfasting. And dressing up, in their Sunday best. Gore chased his wife around for his unpolished shoes, his socks, his Stetson hat, his cream shirt that matched his brown suit. It was not the time they woke up that was the problem, but the pace of their preparations.

The firewood would just not catch. The breakfast of the leftovers from the previous night's supper of *sadza* and fish needed heating. And Gore's wife stopped using her hands every time she opened her mouth. She was a talker of huge stories that continuously cropped up in her small head to find their way out of her small mouth with no disturbance from her hands and legs. Everything about her body was small in contrast to her husband's huge frame. He was a fisherman, whose muscular shape was fit for his job of casting nets and pulling them out of the water with their enormous load of bream, eel and bass. He carried his catch through the forest to his home alone, making several trips to and from the dam at night. He knew the dam area well, as well as he knew his talking wife. The community were aware that he only worked five days a week. His customers had learnt that the business of selling fish only took place very early in the morning, before dawn, at his two-roomed house in the high-density suburb of Katanga in Norton, a town semi-circled by Darwendale Dam.

He spent his Saturdays drinking beer in *shebeens*, but he stopped drinking early in preparation for Sunday. A heavy cigarette smoker, Gore did not indulge in smoking on Sunday mornings before taking Holy Communion. A personal vow that was adhered to religiously.

Gore and MaMoyo were always late for the service. On their way to church Gore took long energetic strides at double the speed of his wife as she trotted behind. Holding the bible to his chest, with his other hand in his trouser pocket, he urged his wife to hurry up.

"We are known for coming late every Sunday – a bad attitude towards the creator and towards those who arrive at church early. Walk, hurry up MaMoyo." But she could not keep pace. Every time they walked the one kilometre to church, the distance between them increased until Gore was out of her sight.

Gore always found a place to locate himself near the back of the school hall the church hired for its services. His loud baritone voice signalled his presence as he sang his lungs out to the Lord. Gore did not need a hymnbook because he knew all the songs by heart, having been born and bred an Anglican. He enthusiastically followed the readings from the Epistles and the Gospels in his bible. If called upon, he could even conduct matins and recite the Creed without hiccup, not to mention the confession prayer and the order of Holy Communion. But he did not belong to the strict sect of Vabvuwi. Genuflecting again and again and kneeling for long periods were not a problem, even for his body of fifty years, but the vows of the Vabvuwi sect of abstinence from alcohol and tobacco were. Gore knew of priests who would puff a cigarette immediately after a church service and of a few who did not hesitate to consume such large amounts of church wine that their sheep were deprived of Holy Communion. "Men born of Adam and Eve are not perfect. Why just throw words at them, why not stones as well?" he would chuckle to challenge the congregation when they questioned the behaviour of some of these men of the pulpit.

One Sunday after church Gore joined the usual company of old time guzzlers. At this time backyard drinking joints selling illicit alcohol had sprouted up all over, as municipal beer halls were not operating and legal alcohol was too expensive and in short supply. Afraid that the drinking hole would be raided by the police at any time, Gore and his friends hastily downed two 750ml bottles of *kachasu*. They parted in very good spirits, their bibles clutched to their chests.

Now alone, Gore walked with his feet wide astride to keep his balance. He staggered along on the side of the road to avoid bicycles and motor cars. He stumbled over tins, stones and other play material left by children. Other road users going and coming his way could not fail to notice the bible-clutching, heavily built Gore as he lurched forwards and backwards. He swore every time his shoes came into contact with one of the objects discarded by the children. The children enjoyed the free show of drunken Mr Gore clutching his bible as he made very little progress in his efforts to get home. "*Vakadhakwa! Vakadhakwa! Vakadhakwa!*" the children taunted. Staggering drunkenly with one hand in the pocket and the other hand clutching a bible to the chest is a precarious endeavour. The body ends up horizontal to the ground. As Gore fell flat on his face, he lost grip of his bible, his other hand not finding time to leave his pocket. The book of God fell with a thud a metre ahead of him.

"Ah! Ah! Ah!" exclaimed the onlookers at the spectacle of the fall of the man of God. They did not immediately come to Gore's help. We rise and fall, rise and fall and rise on our way to heaven. They expected him to rise and stagger on.

"Whose road is this?" Gore growled, his face pitted by the brown gravel that made up the road he had trod. No one got the gist of the drunken enquiry, maybe the devil's road? The children yelled and jumped about him as he struggled to rise. Elders who were not in a hurry joined the children in poking fun at the parishioner.

A teenage boy tried to retrieve the bible from the ground to return to Gore, but he shouted, "Leave my bible alone . . . my bible alone." Gore stumbled forward and landed on the bible before the teenager could pick it up. The fisherman's face, hands, cream shirt and brown suit gathered more soil. His hat that had fallen was delivered to his side by a wire toy truck, driven by a ten-year-old boy with a mischievous grin on his face.

"*Siyana nebhaibheri rangu . . .*" The drunken emphasis discouraged anyone who tried to help. They watched as Gore grasped the bible to his chest with the hand that had eventually managed to free itself from his pocket.

A middle-aged woman recognised Gore the fisherman. She did not attempt to ask the man of God to rise and rise. She sent an SOS message to Gore's marital angel, MaMoyo, who responded without delay, bringing the family wheelbarrow. MaMoyo painstakingly wheeled Gore away, his blotched face covered with his dirty Stetson and his bible clutched to his chest.

A Caged Lion

A caged lion
refuses to roar,
it realises
it's a king no more.
It accepts meat rations,
it is aware
it's not meat for kings.
A caged lion
refuses to rule,
it knows
a cage is no kingdom.
It often purrs,
it understands clearly
it is only a large cat.
A caged lion miaows,
it has concluded
that to roar is for dens
not for cages.

Doves

Here lie two doves
caught
in crossfire
mating
on the boughs of Entumbane.

We Waited

On the day appointed to hold the town council primary elections, we waited. We were a large crowd of about one thousand men and women eager to cast our votes. We waited at the ramshackle buildings on the outskirts of our suburb for the presiding officers from the Party to come and conduct the election. We waited in the hot sun. The huge old gum trees around us had no leaves and their imposing trunks were dying. Women covered their heads with *zambias*, the men with caps. We talked together as comrades. We belonged to the same party. We waited. We joked that the weather had joined the British and the Americans in imposing sanctions on us. The month was February, the month of *mubvumbi*, when, under normal conditions, incessant rains matured our crops. The dry weather was wilting our plants. We did not expect any yields at all from our garden plots. The heat had descended for months and our wells were drying fast. We sat on rubble as we waited, rubble of the buildings destroyed during *Murambatsvina* when the shelters of the poor people who could not construct permanent structures were demolished by the government. We waited, keen to exercise our right to vote in the Goredema town council elections, a fledgling town west of Harare.

We talked in excited, expectant voices as we settled down to wait. We talked about the development programmes that needed immediate attention in our ward, like the water reticulation system that never functioned, the unserviced roads and the lack of electricity. We talked and we waited. We could not understand why we never had access to piped water when our suburb and town were surrounded by dams. Why we had to sink wells when we should have been knee deep in water. We could not work out why the sewer system was not functioning and yet the sewer pipes had been installed before we settled in the suburbs. We waited, appeased by the expectation of being responsible residents who would bring development to the town through the vote.

Hungry and sweaty, we waited, watching the road their cars would come along, munching maize, drinking *freezits*, licking juiceless mangoes and cracking *maputi*. Vendors did a brisk business as we waited and passed the time, confident that the officials would come.

They never came. Some did not wait to chant the slogans to close the meeting. Some went home, tired of waiting. Others waited, raising their fists high and wishing that another election date would be announced soon.

"Don't throw the baby shawl away because the baby has died. Babies, babies are on the way. Comrades. Our party officials are busy conducting elections at many venues throughout Mashonaland West. They must have mixed up the dates. They will come and we will have a chance to choose the candidate who will bring development to our suburb, our ward," a comrade wearing a party T-shirt emblazoned with big black letters 'Power to the people' assured our gathering when he raised his fist to lead a frenzy of sloganeering. The crowd chanted after him, their fists high in the air and their voices loud enough to be heard by the election officials wherever they were. They stamped their feet on the dry ground until a thick cloud of dust mingled with their scattered voices in the air. The time was 5.30pm and darkness was approaching. They left for their homes in excited groups, happy they had taken the first step in developing their new suburb. Then, they waited, expecting the news of the new date for holding the election.

In less than two days another date was announced – the following Saturday. We were glad that the date was soon. Meanwhile the aspiring candidates continued to campaign, issuing maize-meal to residents, converting their personal vehicles into ambulances and hearses, helping the bereaved with money to cover funeral expenses, and paying school fees for less fortunate children. Candidates become strategically benevolent during election time. But it was rumoured the outgoing councillor, Mr Chimbumu, was confident that he would retain the post because the other candidates' curricula vitae had been rejected by the party's election commission. He maintained his silence, avoiding the residents as much as possible, but communicating regularly with the party chefs at the provincial offices. He supplied the officials with eggs and chickens free of charge every week, proceeds from the council land he leased. The top hierarchy of the party appreciated his previous term.

The following Saturday we converged at the usual dilapidated meeting place in song and sloganeering. We sang and the thunderous sound of the cowhide drum summoned those who were still at home to come and vote. We danced in a circle, the well-known *kongonya* dance of whirling and wriggling and raising our bums. The echoes of our voices must have been heard that morning beyond the Nharira hills on the shores of Lake Chivero. At other election venues in the town of Goredema the pattern was repeated: singing, dancing, clapping, and chanting the revered party slogans. Those who did not join in the dance raised their voices high. Noisy expectant voices.

"Chimbumu must go!"

"What has he done for us these past five years?" Most people's votes were secret no more.

"*Murambatsvina* destroyed our homes while we watched like an animal caught in a snare. He did nothing about the destruction of our homes." The woman who made the remarks did not sound angry. Time had healed the hurt that *Murambatsvina* had done in the town.

"Sewage is flooding the streets ... and not even a drop of water comes from our taps. We are billed every month for no services," another big breasted woman shouted as she stepped out in tempo with the drumming to join the dancers who were in a halo of dust.

Vendors seem to realize that every crowd has a golden lining, so as the sun drenched us with sweat, they increased in number, selling melted *freezits* at double the normal price, *maputi*, peanuts, sugar cane, late season mangoes and roasted fresh maize. We ate and we waited. There were no toilets. People just disappeared into nearby plots of wilting maize plants to relieve themselves. There was no water to wash our hands. Residents whose houses were near supplied us with drinking water.

"If I had known, I would have brought some water for sale," one enterprising very tall man said after drinking a free cup of water. Gradually the excitement subsided. The singing stopped. We sat in groups. The long drum now lay on its side to join in the waiting. The expectancy of the morning was wearing out. Some left discreetly. And some asked, "When are these people going to come?" But no one seemed to know. The time was 2.30pm. We ignored the loud question and continued with the weary business of waiting.

"I suspect that the elections are never going to take place . . . something else is going to happen." The voice was low but sounded determined to reveal some unknown truth. A stout *madzibaba*, whose clean shaven head and bushy shiny beard showed the sect of religion to which he belonged, looked around in search of further comments.

"Like what, *madzibaba* . . . you suspect what? Rigging?" an equally stout individual casually asked. Many questions packed in people's heads were waiting to be asked or to be answered.

"Like imposing Chimbumu on us . . .?" The sentence did not see its end because it was intercepted by scowls and grunts uttered by people who were not enjoying the waiting. Words were thrown about, let out by waiting mouths. The words did not sow discord among the residents but they were words of caution. Words that could not remain silent, that could not wait to be said any longer. We agreed that the party could not impose a candidate upon us. The party was resolute on the issue of the choice of candidates. The party would honour the choice of the people.

The electorate waited, but the sun did not. It hurtled towards the western horizon and in no time our watches were reading 5pm. Tongues clicked indignantly. Hands flew about resignedly. We realized that we had spent another day doing nothing. Waiting. Our candidates were no help. They had also spent the day waiting, pressing the buttons on their phones, trying to locate the presiding officers, but the network was bad. Network busy? On voice mail? Not reachable? The provisional electoral commission had not informed them of any postponement. It seemed the electoral party was taking advantage of our naivety.

For a while there was a lull when the one thousand or more residents were consumed by their thoughts. Were the elections ever going to be held? Were the election officials serious? And if they did pitch up at a late hour, were they going to hold the elections? Where we were gathered there were no lights, a consequence of *Murambatsvina*, but, suddenly, the dusty road along which we expected the officials to come was lit up by the arrival of a blue *bakkie* bumping along towards us. We rose like school pupils when their teacher enters the classroom. The passengers of the small truck jumped out of the vehicle before it came to a halt, a splendid show of urgency. Soon we noticed that they seemed to have consumed a considerable quantity of an intoxicating brew. Fists above their heads, they immediately launched into full speed sloganeering. Then we noticed who they were, the Goredema district party chairman, his vice and secretary. Disappointed, we tumbled down onto our seats of rubble. Our resignation was engulfed in the darkness.

The chairman addressed us, "*Tinokukwazisai vabereki,* we are very sorry that we are late in coming to let you know that the election has been postponed to tomorrow. We are asking you, comrades, to assemble here at eight o'clock sharp. The election will definitely take place tomorrow." His drunken voice did not sound sorry. The echo of his voice mingled with our scowls. Two women and a man raised their hands to show that they intended to ask or say something.

"We have been waiting here for two days. What actually is happening?" the first woman asked without chanting the party slogans, a procedure that was supposed to be adhered to without fail. The chairman did not notice. The question was welcomed by many in the multitude, fed up with waiting. We craned our necks, eagerly awaiting the chairman's response. The chairman first looked at his comrades who were standing next to him. Neither of them seemed to know the reason for the delays and postponement of the election. His comrades looked away.

"I . . . I . . . I could tell," he stammered, flabbergasted. The chairman did not expect the residents to confront him with such questions. "I suggest you remain patient . . . come tomorrow." The woman sat down slowly after realizing that no more words were forthcoming from the chairman.

"*Tatenda,*" he hastily thanked the woman. He sounded quite relieved that she had sat down without probing further. "Any more questions?"

"If they do not come tomorrow, what do we do?" questioned another woman, whose voice was thin and weak. I expected her to faint at any moment. She hardly moved her hands or her head.

"We cannot talk about that . . ." the chairman answered, his gaze focused on a man who was raising his hand. The two comrades flanking the chairman nodded their heads in agreement with their colleague's dismissal of the second woman's question.

"When last did you talk to the commissioners?" The man did not wait for the chairman's response before he sat down. He did not expect much from the Goredema district chairman.

"This afternoon, thirty minutes ago," the chairman was quick with the answer. He was in a hurry to finish with us. He clapped his hands together, happy that there were no more raised hands. We looked at each other and signalled with our heads that it was time we dispersed because the district chairman was far from helpful. We rose, mingled for a while and then took our paths home to wait until the next day, Sunday. Slogans that were usually chanted to signal the end of the meeting were not forthcoming. The three officials watched us leave, relief flooding their drunken faces.

By 7.30am the next day, we were already warming the rubble of the election venue with our bottoms. We greeted each other casually, the excitement of the previous day gone. We sat, our eyes fixed on the ground and waited. But time did not wait. 12 o'clock. 2 o'clock, still no election officials.

"Forward with the people!"

"*Pasi nenhunzvatunzva!*" our response was discordant when we were jolted by a loud youthful voice. We livened up and looked at the short man wearing big-rimmed spectacles who was shouting. The man chose to stand in our midst, not in the usual patch reserved for speakers. "Don't you think that it would be better to hold the election on our own? Today, without the commissioners. They are not coming. *Hapana chekumirira apa.*" A bevy of responses flew about as we competed to be heard.

"It is not the procedure . . . party procedure."

"The third candidate is not here . . . Chimbumu is not here . . . how do we handle that?"

"The end result is the same, a candidate of our choice."

"We are not officials!"

"We can hold elections with the candidates who are present, Mandebvu and Chigama. Whoever wins will be our party candidate. The party will accept him." The two aspiring candidates did not utter a single word while we threw suggestions to the floor.

"That is a waste of time," a thick voice resonated resignation. Many people slipped away during the noise of waiting, only about half of the original crowd were left.

"We have wasted a lot of time already!"

A state of confusion followed as many in the crowd started to talk at the same time. There was a shaking of heads as people disagreed with each other. Fingers were pointed. Feet stamped the dry sandy ground and the silent members of the multitude did not know to whom they should listen. The noise was that of people who did not know what to do. People who had waited for too long.

While we made noise, time did not wait with us. Soon the time was 5pm and during the collision of words a 4x4 twin cab with four occupants hurtled up the dusty road followed by the chairman's *bakkie*. The sun was a dark glow to the west of our suburb.

"They have come . . . they have come!" a few words pointedly welcomed the officials and the noise died down. We resumed our seats of rubble. But we knew that the election was not going to be held. The occupants of the 4x4 did not alight from their vehicle immediately. They talked and laughed uproariously. They seemed to be in no hurry. In contrast, the Goredema district party chairman hurried out of his *bakkie*, followed by the outgoing councillor, Chimbumu, who came to stand very near him as if he feared attack. Our candidates remained in our midst. The chairman, as always, rushed through his slogans, which found little response. Mosquitoes were biting us hard. Slaps and claps did not in any way restrain the menacing attack on us.

"*Vabereki tine urombo*, we are late . . . I was waiting for the election officers who only arrived at the community hall a few minutes ago. I realise that you all know them but all the same I will introduce them to you." That was when the officials found it appropriate to join the chairman. They marched slowly in a single file towards him. As it was dark, the driver of the 4x4 left the headlights on, the shiny beams pointing away from us. We waited to hear what they were going to say. We knew that no election was going to be held in the darkness. After the introductions the man we presumed was their leader stepped forward and embarked on sloganeering, which sounded apologetic.

"*Pamberi nemi macomrades! Pamberi nevana vevhu! Pamberi nekunzwisisa!*" he went on and on in a shaky voice until he had exhausted the supply of slogans he knew. He seemed overwhelmed by our calmness and did not see fit to shout the 'down with' part of the slogans.

"We will not delay you further with unnecessary business... the party elections directorate in Chinhoyi, our provincial headquarters, did not approve the candidature of two of the candidates. They are not eligible to contest the council post as their CVs show that they have not held posts in the party. There is no record that they ever held posts even at the cell level. As a result Mr Robert Chigama and Mr Anthony Mandebvu were disqualified and Mr Sekai Chimbumu stands unopposed." The senior official stopped his announcement for a second to determine our response. But before he proceeded to declare Chimbumu the party's candidate for ward 13, a steely woman's voice slit the darkness in a song that seemed to unleash the discontent within us.

> *Povho yaramba, povho yaramba!*
> *Zvemadhisinyongoro*
> *Povho yaramba, povho yaramba!*
> *Zvemadhisinyongoro!*

The multitude immediately joined in the singing. We clapped our hands hard and danced in front of the officials. The senior officer drew back to his colleagues and consulted with the district chairman, who tried to stop the vehement singing by raising his fist to accompany a slogan. We did not respond. We sang and danced, raising dust around us and the officials, who covered their mouths and noses with their palms. After a while the officials withdrew to stand by the chairman's *bakkie* and coughed as if they had been tear-gassed. We did not take any notice of their discomfort.

They talked amongst themselves for some time. No-one joined them, not even the other two candidates who remained inconspicuous in the crowd. The election officials must have misinterpreted our frenzied dancing for a war dance, a warm-up for an onslaught. They went back to their vehicle and drove away with the outgoing councillor. We ululated and whistled to congratulate ourselves on the snub we had executed. Everybody seemed to agree that that was the only way to treat arrogant officials. We had waited too long to accept such an arrangement. We sang and danced.

"*Pamberi neZanu PF! Pasi nenharadada!*"

"Forward with the people's wishes! Down with corrupt leaders!"

A young man forced a roar that interrupted the singing and dancing. "Macomrades, let's go and report this matter to Amai Mondotso. She is the most senior person in the party here in Goredema. She is the town chairperson and a member of the central committee. We cannot wait any longer." Amai Mondotso was a chef as far as party matters were concerned. We agreed that she was the only one who could arbitrate and give us a fair hearing as she was the custodian of the rules and regulations of the party. We hoped she would listen to us. We knew of cadres who, when their grievances were handled unfairly, approached Amai and Amai helped. We realised that going to Amai was not the correct procedure as far as our case was concerned. The person who should have been approached on the matter in the first instance was the district chairman but he seemed to favour the outgoing councillor. We found it appropriate to skip him.

We jogged and toyi-toyied in the darkness to Amai's residence. The suburb was experiencing a blackout due to the daily electricity cuts. Here and there fires decorated the evening as residents cooked supper in their backyards. We sang to the beat of our clattering shoes on the gravel road. In the distance, Nyau small drums could be heard, pervading the darkness with their compact thick sound. The people we met gave way to us, afraid that we were party youths sent out to clobber residents – something that was expected during election time. As we moved along we lost a number of comrades, including one of our aspiring candidates, who had been mysteriously consumed by the darkness.

In less than thirty minutes, we were pushing at the gate of Amai Mondotso's residence, having jogged two kilometres from the high density suburb to the equally dark low density suburb. We stopped when we noticed a moving light inside the house. We maintained a grave silence for several minutes. Eventually Amai Mondotso came out to the porch to find us sitting on her lush lawn. She did not appear perturbed, being used to such visitations. Wearing a long gown, she held a paraffin lamp in one hand, protecting it from the wind with the other. The time was 9pm. A thick odour of beef curry floated in the dark yard. Our hungry stomachs groaned.

"*Macomrades, maswera zvakanaka?*" She was not lavish with slogans even though she was an ex-combatant and senior in the party.

"*Taswera, chef*" we chorused reverently, clapping our hands in greeting.

"*Ndokubatsirai nei macomrades*? Where have you come from?" her voice was calm and sounded receptive. She was a person of the people who welcomed all who came in the name of the Party. We did not respond. Amai did not rush us. She waited for our reply, which was preceded by shifting and shuffling of figures in the darkness.

"*Pamberi neZanu PF! Pamberi nekunzwisisa! Pasi nenharadada!* Down with the people who do not honour the wishes of the*povo*!" the youthful voice roared once more. The young man, a youth leader of Ward 13, took it upon himself to be the first to respond. A firebrand, confident that Amai was a woman of the people continued, "We are from Chikosha and Machembere, Ward 13. The candidates of our choice for the primary council elections have been disqualified by the electoral directorate from Chinhoyi for reasons we do not understand. They are talking about CVs which are not in order – they are imposing someone on us . . ."

"Chimbumu is their man!" This interjection was followed by shouts of excited voices denouncing the way the elections were being held.

"We cannot tolerate such . . ." an excited female voice began before being interrupted by a loud clank as the gate chain was removed. Four policemen kitted out in full combat gear marched through the gate towards Amai.

"Officers can you please deal with this mob. I do not want them in my yard," Amai ordered in a no-nonsense voice. We peered at each other in the darkness. We could not comprehend what was befalling us. We heard what Amai said but could not believe our ears. Something must have gone wrong. Some mistake. Some mix up. We remained where we were as if rooted in the lawn. Amai closed the door behind her and we heard the turn of the key.

"Macomrades, you have heard what the chef said, she does not want you here. Mataka and Chemhere, post yourselves at the gate. We are walking these people to the police station." The two policemen took their positions outside the gate. One by one we rose and wobbled slowly to the gate. "Move comrades. You are under arrest. Do not waste our time." The police officer who appeared to be in charge of the operation pushed those nearest to him as he commandeered us out of the gate.

"Officer, make sure they are all out," Amai shouted from a half opened window. The tone of her voice did not leave any doubt in our minds that we were under arrest.

"Yes chef – move, move, move macomrades."

Pushed by the baton wielding policemen like criminals who had refused to co-operate in an investigation, we stumbled upon each other like cattle being driven into a dip tank. Clicks of tongues were heard and forlorn laughter as we tried to come to terms with what was happening.

"Are we arresting all of them or are we just taking the ringleaders?" Mataka, the huge one, inquired from outside the gate.

"Who is your leader? Who is your leader?" the commanding officer inquired while he secured the gate.

"We do not have a leader," the young man who had initially presented our grievances to Amai roared. As if we had been jolted from a stupor we chorused after him. "We do not have a leader!"

"In that case we are arresting all of you. Do you know your charge?" He sounded intimidating.

"No-o-o-o!" Our response was too loud to leave Amai feeling comfortable. We could see a light move from room to room inside the house.

"You are holding a demo without police permission . . . a serious offence and if you keep on making noise I will charge you for rioting ... now move!" He was angry. Baton sticks descended on our shoulders, heads, buttocks and ribs. The commanding officer was driving us to the police station but his colleagues Mataka and Chemhere were pushing us towards him. Confusion ensued until the commanding officer bellowed, "We are taking them to the police station not the report post." He talked as if his words were exploding from his mouth. At this point more comrades slipped away in the darkness, including the other aspiring candidate. His large frame vanished from our midst. The multitude had shrunk to about eighty, from the one thousand strong crowd that had danced before the election officials.

The police station was about five hundred metres across the Harare–Bulawayo railway line but the policemen ordered us to use the longer route of the tarred road. They feared to lose more culprits if we took the grassy, short cut past the railway station.

A female voice ripped through the darkness in song as we walked along the tarmac, "*Povho yaramba! Zvemadhisinyongoro!*"

We joined in the singing, united in our desire to see justice, although we had not fully recovered from the shock of Amai's handling of our case. We were still confident that the police chief would listen to our story and not charge us. Our actions that day did not warrant our arrest. Moreover, we were ZANU-PF supporters and ZANU-PF supporters could not be arrested for demonstrating. We had never required police clearance. We were doing Party business. We were confident that the Party politburo would not allow this harassment of its supporters. As we approached the police station we sang, clapped our hands and danced. Vehicles slowed down as they approached us and we cordially gave way to them, although we noticed that some drivers panicked. They drove very fast past what they saw as a mob.

We were about 100 metres from the police station on the Harare–Murombedzi road when a pick up truck with one headlight, coming from the opposite direction, rammed into our excited crowd. There was no squeal of brakes, an indication that the driver of the truck had not applied them when he realized that his truck was hurtling towards a crowd. The truck mowed down many people and ended up as a write off in the storm drain beside the road. There were screams and wailing and blood all over the road. Torn flesh and broken bones of a people who had waited. I was one of the lucky ones to escape the human destruction that took place while the policemen looked on.

The front page of the next day's paper read, "A group of ZANU-PF supporters were last night involved in a car accident in Goredema. Seven people died on the spot and several who were seriously injured were ferried to Harare and Parirenyatwa hospitals. Police are investigating the cause of the accident."

It was a very brief piece of news indeed. Very short.

20-044L

The number on my door
reads 20-044L,
but it is not the number
of my house.
The scrap metals
that make the door
include
a motor car number plate.
I regret
any inconvenience caused.

No Funeral

When I die
no gathering
no fires
or chairs around fires
no wake
no gloating
no fussing.
Do not cry
over my carcass.
Do not sigh
over my excesses.
Life is not
what you make it
it is
what it makes
of itself.
Before disposal of my corpse
no vigil
no singing
no drumming
sniffing forbidden
no mourning
no moaning
no speeches
no ceremony
no cadaver viewing
no funeral
no coffin
or tin to contain
my remains.
Shove me in
a hessian sack,
throw it in a deep hole,
cover the hole
with rocks and soil.
Disperse forthwith.

A Buzz

Art does not thrive
on half truths
like politics,
prepare the real thing
honey!

Shonongoro

When you visit a toilet marked 'Free Toilet' in the Sunshine City you are likely to be saluted by a tired looking woman wearing a green dustcoat. At the back of the coat will be written 'City of Harare'. She will be seated on a small five litre tin at the entrance to the toilet, pretending to be cheerful but something about her makes her look miserable.

If she sees that you are an old man she will greet you with "*Masikati vatezvara,*" as if welcoming her father-in-law. Otherwise she might honour you as another relative to draw you in, by calling you daughter-in-law, son-in-law, uncle, mother or aunt. It is not wise to respond to this welcome without preparing for the aftermath, because it is a ploy.

"*Vatete kwatonhora!*" she may utter, reminding you of the cold weather. Who is she to you to give you weather reports? You can feel whether it is cold or not. These conversational gambits are made when you are rushing into the toilet, but, when you come out, it's not about the weather. It's about money.

On exiting the toilet the attendant will bluntly ask you for money to buy lunch or for bus fare, all the time eyeing you like you are a dirty dog that has come to mess up her toilet. She will extend her palm and beg aloud, "*Yese yese ndinowedzera,*" on occasion even going to the extreme of blocking the door to stop you leaving. Those coming into the toilet will be barred from entering even if in desperate need.

The pattern will be repeated in free toilets scattered throughout the city. Most patrons who use these facilities do not answer back, they hurry inside and run away after their business in the lavatory. The accosting voice of the woman trails them in and out of the house of relief. Walking into the toilet to relieve oneself of bodily waste can be quite a trying experience.

On one occasion I encountered a dark, thin woman, her head covered by a fading yellow *doek* with a floral pattern, who, in spite of me telling her that I had no money, insisted on making me pay for her cleaning job.

"*Shonongoro vatezvara!*" the woman accosted me in a loud voice as I entered her territory. Again, at the exit, as I was straightening my clothes before re-entering the outside world, she repeated her demand in a strident voice. *Shonongoro?* She acted like the bride entering the groom's home and pulled me into the scene without my consent. The attendant wanted me to give her money as if she had just married my son? *Shonongoro*, at the door of a municipal toilet?

She even looked down like a shy daughter-in-law, but in reality she was trying to extort money from me. I was not prepared to take the part of father-in-law that she tried to force me to play.

"*Ndatenda*," I thanked her as I negotiated a right turn, trying to sneak away. One lucky bearded man sneaked out while she was concentrating on me.

"*Shonongoro vatezvara!*" she persisted, her eyes now fixed on my face. The city council was paying her. Why was she demanding money from me? Another lanky individual ran past me out of the toilet. He knew the game.

"*Handina.*" I was not lying, I did not have any spare cash, just the correct bus fare for my journey back home. I explained that I regretted that I did not have enough money to pay for her services, and admitted that it was a grievous mistake on my part. She was doing a wonderful job under difficult conditions. I tried to persuade her to leave me alone by spouting such nonsense.

I did honestly appreciate the work she was doing. The floor had a black shine and the smell of the floor polish pervaded the toilet. The toilet was spotless. The cistern was not functioning but she provided users with a five litre plastic bucket full of water for the purpose of flushing the pan. A continuous dribble of water leaked from a pipe into another plastic bucket that had been provided for washing hands, though where the water came from was not clear.

I grabbed her lightly by the waist to move her aside, invading her personal space. "*Makuita seiko imi baba imi?*" she screeched, questioning whether that was suitable behaviour for a father-in-law. She jumped out of my way, offering me an escape route, which I eagerly took.

A Demon

He was ill
the whole year.
He did not die
the whole year.
Chose to succumb
on Christmas Eve
to douse the festive spirit
with sobbing handkerchiefs.
Chose to salt
the sweets and cake
with tears, a spoiler.

Wining and dancing
was
whining and damning.
I wished him hell,
he who
snuffed out the celebrations
with sniffs and sighs.
At our expense of course.
A demon!

Pregnant

I will fall pregnant
I will have a baby.
It is not my blind eyes
nor my crippled legs,
my deaf ears
nor my dumb mouth,
but the belly
that will grow.
I am not giving it
a try,
I am certain
the baby will smile
in the stumps
of my hands,
I will.

A Portrait

There is a picture
in our living room,
a picture hanging
on the wall.
A portrait of myself.
They whisper amongst themselves
the picture is a stunner.
I love it
although I will never
see it
with my blind eyes.
I happen to see it
by chance
only in the hush
of their admiring voices.

The Dread Gentleman

Every morning the dread gentleman came and stood at the same place, along the durawall of Kudzanayi Beer Garden. He looked at the wall as if he was observing some ritual. Every day he touched the durawall at one corner, mesmerized by something I could not see. He talked to himself, shook his head and threw his hands about as if in unsuppressed rage. I watched him every morning while I waited for transport to Harare. *Kombis* that plied the Norton-Harare route on the Bulawayo road took so long to arrive that I had plenty of time to watch. All us commuters stood at the bus terminus, popularly known by the residents of Norton as Katanga, for long hours. Even if we arrived at Katanga as early as 5am, we could wait until 8am before we managed to get on any transport. Most commuters to Harare had given up hope of ever arriving at work on time because transport was so hard to come by. Fuel was in short supply and government was continually 'in the process' of sourcing foreign currency to buy the precious liquid.

The man sported a white beard and long hair that he kept in a woollen pouch that hung at the back of his head. He always wore a dark brown work-suit. Whenever he walked towards his place by the durawall, he strode in hurried business-like steps, but, when he arrived at the spot, he stopped and looked around as if he was lost. Hands stuck in the shallow pockets of his jacket, he circled the place several times, oblivious of the busy main road three metres away. Passers-by just glanced at him and proceeded to get on with their daily errands. Across the road, vendors in the fish and vegetable markets went about their business without giving any attention to what the man did. But I noticed him. Did he enjoy visiting the dirty wet place beneath the huge *Muhacha* tree? The uncomfortable smell of *Muhacha* tree wafted over us commuters as we patiently waited. Perhaps his ceremonies every morning were part of a ritual? Certain Shona tribes did revere this tree.

One bright Monday morning he came carrying a high wooden stool and an umbrella. He sat on the stool with his back to the durawall and opened the umbrella above his head. From where I stood in the queue I could see that his lips were moving as if he was talking or singing to himself. I concluded that if he was singing, it was not a happy song. He sat like he was watching the passing traffic while he talked to himself. I developed a sudden urge to know what he was saying, but a *kombi* with space arrived and I pushed my way on.

One rainy morning he brought a big canvas beach umbrella. He stood beneath the umbrella, defying the pounding summer downpour while we scrambled for shelter below a small overhang. He stood there as if nothing was happening. My curiosity about him was now beginning to be shared by many in the queue. Transport was becoming rarer and we spent longer and longer with little to do but watch the goings on at the durawall. We were quite disappointed that day when a long-awaited bus came along to take us away from watching him. When I returned in the evening I did not see him, he must have left before sunset. I did not see him or his stool and umbrella. Darkness had descended and he would have finished whatever business he was involved in. At times he talked as if he was talking to someone else, as if he was a shopkeeper. He would look around and stretch his hands out hopelessly as if to indicate that he had nothing left. He would talk as if he was chatting to a customer who was inquiring about some item in a shop. His gestures seemed polite.

One Monday morning people in the queue were silently singing the Monday blues and repeatedly yawning as we waited for a bus that was not forthcoming, when I saw the dread gentleman come to his customary place dressed in a black suit. The dreadlocks hung at the back of his head in smart shiny black waves. A white shirt was too conspicuous to remain unnoticed below the black tie. He carried a briefcase made of dark brown leather. It looked expensive. I later noticed that he held a fat chequebook in his other hand. He came to claim his place in the queue, but he insisted that he wait in his usual position beside the durawall. I could not fathom why he did not put his chequebook away in the briefcase. He held the chequebook as if it was part of his outfit. He wrote a few things in a notebook he took from the briefcase and looked around. He seemed to be taking stock of imaginary things. Eventually he bade farewell to his durawall and joined the queue two metres behind me.

He looked self-assured, greeting the bored commuters reservedly. He kept cocking his head backwards, a ritual I followed with increasing curiosity. I wished that he was standing nearer to me so that I could strike up a conversation with him. When a *kombi* came there was pandemonium as the crowd tried to scramble through the small doorway. I noticed that he, like I, was one of the very few commuters who remained where they stood. He did not join in the fight to get in the *kombi*. He just shook his head and seemed to feel pity for the desperate commuters.

An empty eighty-seater bus came soon after the *kombi*. I forwent my favourite spot by the exit window to share a seat with him. He sat upright after cleaning the seat with a tissue. He immediately opened his briefcase, the colour of which matched his elephant skin shoes, and brought out a calculator, the size of a small laptop.

"I order everyone on this bus to keep quiet because we are in an office," a pot-bellied man with eyes high up his forehead shouted with assumed authority when the bus started to move. He was known to provoke heated discussions amongst commuters, talking continually until the forty kilometre journey from Norton to Harare was over. This time he had picked on the dread gentleman who was busying himself with numerous calculations of figures he read from a list written on a piece of paper. Someone I did not recognise commented in a low unsteady voice, "A briefcase businessman can do business anywhere."

The dread gentleman did not raise his head or hint that he heard what anyone said. Most of the people in the bus were quiet and listening, because the commuters knew Pot-Belly, who wore a short and a very broad tie that appeared like a baby feeder. They knew his pranks and they welcomed the free entertainment he provided on the boring daily trips from Norton to Harare.

"He is okay because he was not affected by the tsunami," Pot-Belly, who sat reclining back to give room to his stomach, shouted. Tsunami was the wanton destruction of buildings by the government, named after the tsunami that devastated East Asia and Africa. The passengers roared with laughter, which Pot-Belly clearly enjoyed. He loved making people laugh at other people's expense.

"He was affected. His illegal structure was destroyed," a young man who wore a baseball cap joined in. He talked from a seat just behind ours. Most emergent business people had their place of work destroyed in the wave of politically motivated destruction carried out by government to weed out dissent among the urban populace.

"He was not affected. The briefcase business is an illegal structure . . . they missed him." There was a fervent uproar but it failed to arouse the dread gentleman who was engrossed in his figures. At times his lips moved, complemented by the nodding of the head.

"But his business premises were not spared!" the baseball youth insisted. Perhaps he knew the dread gentleman? Pot-Belly held the back of the seat in front of him with his stubby hands as if he wanted to rise from his seat. He was quiet for a short time while he thought up the right words to utter in response. Despite the shouting and laughing the dread gentlemen kept himself busy, seemingly oblivious that he was the subject of the noise in the bus. Or, if he knew, he ignored it and pretended to concentrate on his figures. He may not have been interested, yet nearly everyone else in the bus found the repartee fascinating.

"Does that tell us that he is not now an illegal structure?" Pot-Belly responded. "He is still operating. Can't you see he is busy?"

Other passengers in the bus started to join in.

"Although our tsunami was manmade, it really had some devastating effects on the terrain and on the welfare of everybody. We should also ask for international aid in such times. Zimbabweans contributed a lot towards the tsunami disaster of East Africa and Asia. Our tsunami destroyed all things that were made without plans."

"You mean God created the briefcase business people without approved plans like he created other people?"

I realized that the dread gentleman sighed every now and then, as if he was releasing some tension.

"Yes . . . There are no plans . . . They are illegal structures . . . Head over body like those condemned buildings with asbestos over brick. But he is not smart like Samanyika the chef who works at a five star hotel . . . How can he be illegal . . . an . . . an illegal structure?"

It seemed no time at all before the bus turned into Chinhoyi Street from Samora Machel Avenue. We had arrived in Harare, forty kilometres from where we boarded the bus. Forty kilometres of the 'Pot-Belly amusement show'. The passengers disembarked still in stitches. And the talking and the laughing did not in the least help in satisfying my curiosity. Instead I left the bus more curious, wishing I had heard more about the gentleman sitting next to me. I decided to follow him for as long as time to start work permitted. He walked slowly along the streets of the city centre window-shopping as he gazed at electrical goods shops and at wristwatch shops.

Work meant that I had to postpone my research on him until late that evening, when I hoped to see him at the durawall back in Norton.

The sun was still up at 5.30pm that day when I got down from the bus at Katanga shopping centre, back from work. A rare feat. On the grey concrete durawall there was a notice written in white paint. A brush had obviously not been used to write the notice but a finger dipped in paint. The lettering was not large but could be read from where I stood.

'Sams Electrical Investment, we buy and sell all electrical goods. We repair stoves ions, hitters and all domestic and industry requirements. And all kinds of risk watches.' I understood the notice in spite of the spelling mistakes.

While I was musing upon the writing on the wall, the dread gentleman arrived. He had changed into a very light brown tracksuit, the colour matching his complexion. He stood beside me.

"Please excuse us," he ordered me in a desperate voice. I did not know how far further back I was to stand, I was already three metres away from him. I looked about and around him to ascertain how many of 'us' there were. He was carrying a small aluminium bucket of water. Three men in white robes then appeared from around the corner of the beer hall. Their heads were clean shaven, an abundant application of petroleum jelly made their heads shine.

"This is the place." He made four long strides along the durawall and three long strides away from the durawall.

"Let us pray." The three men knelt side by side, the oldest of them, who knelt in the middle, holding the bucket of water. The dread gentleman took a few moments of thought, perhaps he did not know if he was supposed to follow suit. He eventually decided to squat behind the *Vapostori*. The three of them sported thick white beards that showed that a lot of effort had been taken to keep them clean white. I moved a little further away but still within hearing distance.

People began to assemble and watch. And the juke-box blared *sungura* music from behind the durawall. The three white robed men placed their hands on the bucket. The elder in the middle opened the prayer in a loud voice, "In the name of the Father, the Son and the Holy Spirit." The other *Vapostori* joined in the prayer with vehemence. Each prayed at his own speed in his own words. Their eyes were tightly closed.

"The Lord God of all men, giver of all life, take heed of our prayers. We beseech you to hear us when we pray. Through your son Jesus Christ you fed the five thousand, the seven thousand, and they were filled. You turned water into wine. You have the love of your people at heart, grant this your child grace that he may operate his business in peace."

The juke-box kept churning *sungura* music above the loud voices of the apostles.

"When you created Man, you wanted him to enjoy the fruits of your mercies. Your desire is not for man to suffer. Destroy the machinations of the bad spirits, goblins and demons sent by the devil to destroy your son's business. His endeavours are genuine and faultless. Destroy those who plan the downfall of your child. You promised with them great mercies that you will make his enemies his footrest and stool. You shall raise him above them and he shall reign over them forever and ever." When I looked at the dread gentleman his eyes were wide open. His arms were clasped at the chest. His mouth was shut.

"Good God, your son, oh Lord, that his enemies may be vanquished. His children are hungry because the devil has destroyed their livelihood. Our sons and daughters sleep out in the cold because the devil has removed all shelter from around and above them." One of the *Vapostori* was certainly becoming personal. It seemed his home had been destroyed as an illegal structure during the destruction that swept the country, the tsunami.

"These *Vapostori* are on a conversion mission. They no more pray in the forests or mountains like Johane their founder did. One of these days we may partake of wine with them in the beer garden." These were the words of a drunk man who had come out of the beer garden as if he had just been sent to comment on the proceedings along the durawall. He soon staggered his way back in search of more beer.

"This ground be blessed in the name of the Father, the Son and Holy Spirit. May the Lord God also bless the enterprise. May the public see good in the goods that will be sold here. Amen."

The elder rose and sprinkled the holy water from the bucket to exorcise and purify the place. Some drops fell on my trousers and black shoes.

"You shall wash your body with the remainder of this water for six days," the elder instructed the dread gentleman and, with a show of abundant authority, handed him the bucket. The dread gentleman received the bucket with both hands and drew it to his chest. The *Vapostori* left immediately without formalities. They marched away in single file and did not look back.

The crowd of onlookers dispersed. I couldn't discern the expression on their faces because it was getting dark. But I heard moans of sympathy directed at the dread gentleman below the loud music beyond the durawall. I concluded that the people desired the prosperity of the dread gentleman. They appreciated his efforts, however small, after such provocation by the authorities. They were peace-loving people who did not retaliate with violence. They did not believe in the old law – an eye for an eye. They did not believe in destructive engagement.

They knew that the authorities destroyed their homes, factories, offices, stores, butcheries and whatever they had without giving them alternative accommodation. They destroyed their small vending markets, their livelihood, without compensation. They knew that government was a soulless machine that did not have blood flowing through its veins. That had no eyes. No ears. That had no heart.

The dread gentleman rose from where he squatted, made a few grunts like a sated dog after partaking of a rare delicacy. He put the bucket on the ground and clapped his hands once. He picked up his bucket by the handle and left me to make my way home. On my way I contemplated the success of the purification exercise. The exorcising exercise.

The next day, while I stood in the bus queue, I saw the dread gentleman arranging his wares for display, new and second hand on a metal table. The goods ranged from watches and electrical gadgets to electrical components of all shapes and sizes. A big red and white picnic umbrella was pitched over his head from a wooden pedestal. He wore a spotless white dustcoat on top of a blue shirt and cream trousers, and he was whistling a joyful gospel song. I saw people come to the table to enquire and to buy. I wished him well and a prosperous life ahead after the devastating tsunami that left the landscape for all of us flattened. A survivor.

At the Bus Station

When you arrive
at the bus station
pull down your tie
or remove the tie
to prevent strangulation.
During the fight
to board the bus,
unfasten all buttons
of the shirt and jacket
to avoid losing the buttons.
During the battle
to gain entry
to the bus,
tighten both shoelaces
for, when you are hauled
into the bus,
you hang in the air
and the shoes may come off,
tighten your belt
to avoid being undressed
during the scrambling
at the door,
remove your spectacles
and hold tight to someone
until you are in the bus.
During the climb
pay no attention to human sounds,
also bear in mind
words lose meaning
until you are inside the bus.

Candy Mercenaries

When the judge granted the divorce
I did not know
it was the beginning
of a fierce long battle.

Our children became spies
who could cross the line,
infiltrate either camp,
find information about
the goings on in enemy camp.

The little combatants
also became artillery
after a divorce treaty
that never brought us peace.

Hired for candy
the little mercenaries
devastated our separate lives
because we were ex-spouses
we desired that
they become ex-children.

Second Look

Why are you turning
your head?
Did you not see
from my back
that I am on crutches?
You are not sure
of your vision,
you need a second look?
Sooner or later
you will require
crutches for your eyes.
Spectacles.

The Toilet Issue

We decided that we had to treat the toilet issue with urgency. We had not met to resolve the matter because we, the eleven lodgers at Marimo's residence, were not brave enough to call a meeting. A visit to the toilet did not bring relief to the user, instead it led to misunderstandings that often developed into fistfights. Some lodgers even decided to use toilets elsewhere. Beer hall toilets, church toilets or nearby bushes.

The first incident was an encounter between Marubber and me. He beat me with thoroughness, making sure I lost two teeth and that I was out of action for seven days. My whole body ached like I was run over by an elephant. I could not bend my knuckles. Even my tongue moved only when it was really necessary. I admitted secretly that I would never be Marubber's match.

My crime was that I went into the toilet when Marubber's wife was inside. I only discovered that she was there when I was already inside the ramshackle outhouse. I had edged in sideways as the entranceway and short passage to the seat were too narrow to allow anyone to turn. And the woman did not warn me when she heard me walk in. Anyway, I would not have been able to turn even if she had warned me.

Marubber's wife cried out loud like she was about to be raped, which prompted Marubber to rush to investigate. He found me sliding out of the toilet crabwise. Without asking any questions, he yanked me out, vice-gripped and punched me several times in the face and head. When he released me I fell against the side of the building, where he kicked and trampled me. He did not say a word. He was a man of action, physically orientated. Marubber feared no one at the residence except Saddam, another no-nonsense lodger. They had never crossed swords. I wonder why they never met in the damned toilet. My fellow lodgers did not find my thrashing sufficient enough reason to meet to resolve the toilet issue.

The most recent unfortunate person to run into trouble was Patches. On that day we seriously decided to do something about the toilet issue. Patches had drunk beer the night before at a *shebeen* and came home early in the morning towing a sack full of *scuds*. He invited us to join him in his pursuit. Soon he had a company of other lodgers – free beer chancers – around him.

On his fourth trip to the dark toilet Patches staggered into it sideways without caution. Not noticing that someone was seated on the toilet, Patches drunkenly sprayed the occupant with a jet of his urine. The jet did not switch itself off immediately when Patches realized his mistake. Instead he drunkenly swore at the man and it was only after the damage was done that he recognised Saddam.

The toilet was not a *Blair toilet* or a pit toilet. It was a structure that was built by someone who had no respect for the call of nature. The small building had no windows. Its low roof forced the user to stoop forward when urinating. Although there was no door, no light beam lit the cubicle at the end of the narrow passage. Farm bricks supported an asbestos roof that was weighed down by big rocks. The pan was so low you could only sit comfortably with your legs stretched forward. The floor was rough and sandy. We took turns to clean the toilet everyday, but a thick stench persisted and big green flies threatened to attack anyone who came inside.

When Patches eventually deposited his manhood where it belonged, he apologized, "I am sorry . . . I did not see clearly . . . I did not know . . ." Patches' voice suddenly betrayed his nervousness as the big man hurriedly pulled up his trousers.

"You did not see what . . . what?" Jairos was his name but the many gamblers with whom he spent his time called him Saddam on account of his furious fists. A bad loser who beat his fellow gamblers until they surrendered their gains to him. There was never any resistance to his dictates. Weaklings hired him to recover their money from small time bullies who refused to pay their debts.

When we heard the growl we trooped to the toilet but we did not venture in. We knew Saddam was not only a barking dog but also a biting bulldog.

"I am sorry . . . I made a terrible mistake . . ."

"In my face? In my face?"

We heard thumps against the wall, and the thuds and groans of a person receiving heavy punishment. The toilet seemed overcrowded by just two people.

In no time at all Saddam stormed out, his face wet and dripping urine. We made way for him to pass as he rushed to the makeshift bathroom of plastic sheets and gum poles. There was no water in the bathroom so he took a five litre metal pail from his room and drew water from a well that was sunk near the lavatory. We, as well as Saddam's wife, watched nervously as Saddam rushed about. We guessed the cause of the havoc in the latrine. Patches did not come out.

"Someone should see what is wrong with Patches inside there . . ." suggested a drunken companion who held a *scud* tightly to his chest. He peeped inside and called, "Patches, Patches. I cannot see a thing . . . Patcheeeeeeees come out!" Patches did not respond. We did not know whether he was ignoring the calls because he hated to be called that name or because he was badly hurt. His real name was Mathias.

I volunteered to retrieve him from the toilet. Wedged between the toilet wall and the seat, he was bleeding from his mouth and his nose. The only matchstick I had died out but I had seen how he was positioned. He could not see the hand I extended to him, so I decided to first dislodge him from his cramped position by pulling him by the legs. At the entrance someone helped me to squeeze him out of the passage. By then the landlord had joined the lodgers in watching the crabwise rescue operation.

"He did not wreck my toilet?" Marimo asked as if the lavatory was a decent structure. "Mathias, why do you spoil your life by drinking too much?" The landlord was not worried about the damage to Patches. "Look at him . . . he looks aged . . . older than me . . . you did not wreck my toilet?" Marimo asked again, peering into the dark toilet.

"No baba-a-a," the bleeding Patches replied as he crawled slowly to his room, which was situated behind a mango tree. His drinking mates did not help him to his feet; instead they joined

Marimo in mocking him. Patches was only seen walking steadily, though with a slight limp, five days later.

"Last time it was me." An impromptu meeting started immediately Patches disappeared into his room. Marimo was still making miserable remarks about Patches when I started to narrate my ordeal at the hands of Marubber.

"We are lucky that our landlord is here. We are not talking about the fights but we are talking about what causes the fights." Saddam and Marubber were not present.

"The toilet requires a proper door," Masimba, a young lodger, chipped in.

"There is not enough light inside the toilet. I use a candle to do the cleaning even during the day," I said, remembering the incident that cost me two teeth. Marimo smiled to show that he was really enjoying the discussion.

"The toilet is too narrow ... the seat you ... the pan ... the roof ... the thing needs total refurbishment!" an excited guzzler declared.

Marimo laughed sarcastically and strutted towards us. "You are a funny lot. You people are now telling me what to do at my homestead ... how I should run my affairs?" As he gazed at us, his mouth toyed with a weird smile.

"We feel that you will understand if you listen to our grievances," one member of our group said in a low voice.

"What problems ... you guys tell me?" He sounded as if he was chatting with a group of street children.

"We need decent accommodation which includes the toilet facility."

"Whistle or sing before you enter to alert anyone inside of your intentions," he retorted as he waited for our response.

"No!" we chorused. Whistle? Sing? Like he did not know that toilet business required one's full attention.

"Are you in full view of other people when you are using the toilet?"

"No," I rushed to answer in an effort to make him agreeable to some of our demands.

"That was the toilet I used when I came here with my family. The rooms in which you are lodging are the ones I occupied before I built my house." He pronounced the words 'built my house' with pride, as he turned his head to admire the unfinished structure. "I never complained." We laughed heartily but soon wrapped up our laughter as we noticed the sneer on his face.

"You people do not want a landlord who does not harass you... you..." he spluttered, foaming at the mouth. "If you continue with this useless talk in my yard I will... you will vacate forthwith. Now disperse!" He clicked his tongue once and we disappeared into our rooms. Silence descended on the residence except for the whimpering of Patches who was in extreme physical torment. Those who had unfinished *scuds* drank them behind closed doors.

Drunk

In the photograph
I was so drunk
that I would stagger
out of the picture.

This is Harassment

In the heat of the day
glaring billboards
blind my eyes with orders.
At night neon lights
with overwhelming colours
instruct me to fly
the airline that cares,
drive the millennium car,
watch the film of the year.
This is offending.
Command me to save
with the bank
of the people,
insure your life,
invest for your future.
This is alarming.
Buy at factory price. Buy.
Buy imported fabric. Buy.
Buy genuine leather. Buy.
This is harassment.

Slogans

Their slogans are scattered
like their tattered voices,
for their bellies
are empty pantries
full of disturbed dust.

The Score

The match began at 2pm one hot Sunday. The teams, Hammers United and Portland Cement Hurricanes, had warmed up excitedly, flexing their muscles for five minutes before the match started. A show of stamina. The fans, who stood expectantly along the touchline, stamped their feet and cheered on their teams. Mabvuku Stadium had no terraces. It was the final match of the season for the two leading teams in the league. Bets had been placed privately without the interference of bookmakers. It was the match anxiously awaited by the residents of the suburb. Blue shirts and white shorts for Hammers, yellow shirts and black shorts for Portland. A colourful match. The referee in his white shirt and black shorts jogged enthusiastically to the centre of the pitch, and the assistant referees patrolled the touchline with their white flags at the ready. The ball bounced at the correct pressure. A white and brown ball with a tube. We had not yet caught on to tubeless football technology. The skin of the ball consisted of leather patches stitched together with laces.

The referee's first whistle was full of breath. The motorists who were watching the match from their cars hooted their hooters. It was a significant event. A place to be on a Sunday afternoon in those days of scarce entertainment. I, and my company of drinkers, sat behind one of the goal posts, which had no nets, enjoying our five litre container of beer and the game.

The game was fast moving with a lot of knocking of thighs, clashing of ankles and kicking of shins. The referee was quick to blow his whistle when he spotted a foul, but many fouls went without reprimand. It was a closely fought game, but with the Hammers having the upper hand as far as style and possession of the ball were concerned. Unexpectedly, ten minutes into the game, a Portland Cement striker, Madziwa, dispossessed a complacent Hammers' full back, Masango by name, just outside the box and unleashed a whistling shot past the Hammers' goalkeeper. The jubilant Portland fans went into an early celebration. The referee's whistle confirmed the score, but one of the assistants waved his flag determinedly. In an instant, Hammers' fans thronged the pitch. "No. No. No goal," they chanted. It was not uncommon those days for supporters to show their disappointment by coming onto the pitch in the hope of forcing the referee to change his decision. The Hammers' team surrounded the referee complaining about his decision, threatening him. Refereeing can be a dangerous undertaking. During the mayhem, the Hammers' goalkeeper brought the football tube, still full of pressure, from behind the goal to show the referee. The Hammers' number five brought the leather outer skin of the same ball from near the penalty spot. The referee could not understand what had happened. Hurrying across the pitch, the assistant referee who had raised his flag came to explain. "The lace that had joined the leather patches together must have snapped as Madziwa kicked the ball. The inner tube went past the goalkeeper but the skin only went as far as the penalty spot. What is your decision?"

What could the referee do? He had already blown his whistle to indicate a goal, but the Hammers' players and fans were in a threatening mood. But he could not reverse his decision, a move that would obviously upset the Portland Cement players and fans.

"I will have to postpone this match until next week. I do not have a spare ball," the referee declared in a very shaky voice, and trotted off the pitch flanked by his assistants.

I Lost a Verse

I was immersed
in working a poem
when a briefcase businessman
whom I shared a park bench with
received a call
through his cell phone,
a business call
I presumed.
He borrowed the pen
I was scribbling with,
I lost a verse
he got an order.

Greetings

Those days gone,
good morning, good afternoon
and good evening
were announced loud and clear,
a salute
to all we met.
Amenities of togetherness
are bothersome
these cumbersome days.
In the morning
we moan,
the good of good morning
does no good.
In the afternoon
we froth,
the good of good afternoon
does not make it
out of the mouth.
In the evening
we whine,
the good of good evening
hurtles out
as if good and evening
were chasing each other
out of the mouth
and in how do you do
we grit our teeth
to greet our kith
grating a greeting.

Tired Feet

A man arrived
in a park,
kicked off shoelace-less shoes
from his fetid feet.
Tired feet stared
at a notice written –
'stay off the grass'.
Lush grass sneezed,
the smell of dirty feet
choked its shoots.
The legs bent and creaked –
we cannot go further.
The man dropped
to sleep
on an empty stomach.

Our Boss

He was our boss. We feared him. We did not respect him. One of the reasons was that he used his right boot to send his instructions home. His boot had even lost its shape after landing on our buttocks so many times. We always stood a safe distance away during morning job allocation parades. It was certain that when he warned that he would jump on us, he would do so. Working for him was an experience fraught with danger.

"The country is poor because of you lazy people." Sometimes his diatribes hit home as the work on the farm did not always keep us busy for the whole of the day. "Zimbabwe is hungry. I do not want this farm to be repossessed because you bastards do not work. I am not bringing in extra labour. You lot will have to do the job." Maramba was always in a harsh mood during parade. He must have believed that his temper propelled us to produce. Produce what? He was absent from the farm for many days on Party business. During his absences we sometimes did work until our muscles ached but he never seemed to appreciate our efforts. I think he imagined us stealing things that were not there, things that he wished were on the farm.

The farm was littered with broken equipment. Two tractors (non-runners), spent pick heads, hoes and shovels with no handles. Pieces of broken down cultivators. Heaps of rusted pipes. The old *Land Rover*, which the so-called farm manager drove around, always had to be push started. There was virtually no reliable equipment.

Even though the green revolution was at stake, the boss did not plant the wheat that he had intended to grow that winter. His excuses were endless: the Grain Marketing Board did not pay him for the previous summer crop, the banks had no money to lend . . . But there was work to be done in spite of the problems; work that had to be carried out by the labour force that had dwindled to eight men and three women. The main occupation that winter was tree-felling, for firewood to sell to residents of the nearby town. A bonus of the numerous power cuts. We also cut thatching grass for people building gazebos.

"We did not have much ammunition when we liberated the country. We had to make do with what was there. *Nharadada dzevanhu.*" The barrage was accompanied by a lot of spitting. Maramba's mouth produced a stream of saliva during the morning parade.

At times we believed he sincerely meant business, that he was trying to revive a derelict farm. The previous 'farmer' had allowed the farm to fall into the poor state in which Maramba found it, engaging in no farming activities for three years. When he did visit the farm he brought a host of friends, who would drive around the farm and end up having a picnic on the verandah of the farmhouse. He was however generous with his money and bought us packets of *matemba*, bars of soap, maize-meal, salt and cooking oil. For remaining at his farm and for taking care of his property, he gave us a few dollars each month. Each time he left the farm he addressed us in the presence of his entourage, telling us his grand plans like a politician campaigning for votes. He was different to Maramba who was always quick to say, "If you continue to laze around I will throw you off the farm." Maramba knew we had nowhere to go at short notice, the neighbouring farms had no work. The reasons they gave for producing little were varied: the 'sanctions' imposed by the West, the Grain Marketing Board not paying for grain delivered to its silos, the government being late in issuing handouts like seed, fertilizer, diesel and agro-chemicals. All the farmers sang the same song.

Yet our farm had, courtesy of Maramba's connections, stacks of fertilizer, which was delivered at night and neatly stored in a large windowless tobacco barn. Although there was not much work to be done during the day, some of us found ourselves doing unscheduled jobs in the thick darkness.

Late one night a tractor towing a trailer arrived at the farm. We knew Shumba, the driver, was from a farm ten kilometres away, but we could not figure out the purpose of his visit, until

Maramba gave three of us, the chosen few, our instructions outside the tobacco barn.

"Load the bags of fertilizer onto the tractor. Take a knife with you to open the bags. Our tractor driver will show where I want you to put the fertilizer. Now get on with it. I will pay you your bonus as I always do." He always paid us immediately after such night work was done. Maramba was never in a harsh mood during these hush hush jobs.

He stood in silence for a while and watched us load the tractor. We, the chosen few and our tractor driver Mudzanga, loaded the bags swiftly. Shumba stood puffing his cigarette, seemingly unconcerned at how the operation was being conducted. But we knew how such jobs were handled, discreetly. In no time the tractor was full of fifty kilogram bags of fertilizer.

"Mudzanga, you must drive the tractor because you know the fire guard road well. Be careful, that thing is on hire!" Mudzanga was so excited at the prospect of driving a working tractor that he immediately jumped onto the driving seat. I could see his face shine as he swung the steering wheel. He did not hear the sound of appeal in his master's voice. It was a long time since he had driven a tractor. He held the wheel as if the vehicle was already in motion.

"*Imi vemiromo mirefu*! Jump onto the tractor!" We knew that this was an undercover operation and that Maramba was trusting us not to give him away by talking about the job to anyone else. By farmworker standards, we were paid handsomely for these clandestine tasks. Amongst the jobs we had been asked to do in the dead of night were collecting hard-to-come-by diesel from secret locations, collecting and delivering bags of government-issue seed, moving irrigation piping from farms that had recently been liberated from white settlers, and even loading pit sand onto big trucks.

"I will take you back to the compound where you can sleep," Maramba informed Shumba.

"But . . . my boss told me that I am not allowed to let any other person drive this . . .'" Shumba didn't finish his sentence because Maramba's palm slapped across his face. Shumba held his ground, coolly holding on to the steering wheel with one hand from where he stood beside the tractor.

"Your boss knows about this arrangement. He knows." Maramba's voice sounded desperate.

"I'll phone my boss to verify." Shumba threw away the cigarette he was smoking and reached into his shirt pocket. Our boss raised both palms before the driver in a gesture of supplication. Shumba continued to fish out his cell-phone.

"Now you are delaying us. It is getting late. I will give you ten dollars for your trouble, ten American dollars." He forced the note into Shumba's hand. "There is beer in my fridge, you can have as many as you want when we get back to the house." The boss's voice was filled with anxiety. He obviously did not want the job to fail. Maramba sighed with relief when Shumba put the phone back into his shirt pocket. "Come with me . . . your beer," he said, leading Shumba by the hand towards his *Prado*, worried that he might change his mind. A few minutes later the driver heard the distant drone of his boss's tractor as he sat on a stool in Maramba's kitchen. He smiled to himself as he topped up his glass with more cold beer from Maramba's fridge. He thought no more about his boss's order.

The tractor loaded with fertilizer bumped along for about 500 metres to a fireguard path that ran along a stream. Mudzanga, who knew the road well, travelled fast, turning the wheel as if he was dodging boulders in his path. We had to caution him to slow down because we were in danger of being thrown out into the stream. We jolted to a halt at the big farm dam, where a silver gleam of moonlight shone on its surface. Because Maramba had not given us details of our job, we were flabbergasted to see Mudzanga heave a bag of fertilizer into the shallow waters of the dam before ripping it open with his knife.

When he came out of the dam, holding the empty bag, he instructed us, "That's exactly what we are going to do with all the bags. Let's get on with it, we still have two more trips after this." His tone was full of authority. Mudzanga was always like that when the boss was not around.

We formed a line and threw the bags from the tractor to each other and finally to Mudzanga, who was waist deep in the water. He cut the bags with the knife as if he was slashing at the bellies of animals attacking him. We made three quick trips, dumping each tractor load of fertilizer at different places in the dam. We burnt the empty sacks in a hidden cave.

"We do not want to leave any traces behind," the tractor driver cum supervisor cum labourer warned us. We knew the job had been well executed when we made our final inspection of the dam. All 150 bags of fertilizer had dissolved, leaving no clue.

Maramba paid us at 3 o'clock that morning when we returned from the job. Later that morning we saw him driving his *Prado* away from the farm, smiling. A few days later the newspaper reported searches of many farms as part of the investigation into the abuse of the Government's input support scheme. Maramba's connections had warned him well.

Doubt

Those courting days, Juliet,
your virgin breasts
pointed at my chest
at my heart
and seemed to assure me
'It is you
you I love.'

These days I have doubts
despite your repeated assurances
that you care for me –
your breasts pointing down
at that toothless child.

Shortages

Certain people
are like shortages,
they disappear
only to appear
under new labels
like some women
from honeymoon.

Wrong

Everything I do is wrong
I am so wrong
I say wrong things
I am so wrong
I sing wrong tunes
So wrong
I should stop thinking
Wrong things
So wrong
I belong to the wrong trade
So wrong
I pray to the wrong God
So wrong
I father the wrong children
So wrong, wrong
I reflect upon
A wrong thought,
That I chose a wrong life.

Murehwa

Chipikiri and Chizema, who had washed and clothed the deceased, came and reported to the elders that they had finished their task. There was no comment from the elders, who had assigned one elder and two relatives of the deceased to carry out the task. The two men took their seats by the dwindling fire of logs. A chilly but calm day, the old men found comfort around the fire. The burial was scheduled to take place soon after lunch, the *chirariro*.

"Where did you leave Mapako?" Mukoko, one of the elders, asked when he noticed that old Mapako, who had been assigned to oversee the washing of the body, was not with the other men. Cleansing of the departed was done with reverence. It required know-how and people of strong mind.

"He remained behind..." Chizema spoke quietly and hesitantly, throwing a quick glance at his colleague, who did not pay much attention to what he was saying. They seemed not to want to discuss the undertaking.

Mukoko swung round in his seat to face the two men. The other elders stopped talking, something was amiss. What now, they asked themselves silently. They had assumed that the washing of the deceased was finished, judging by the time Mapako and his colleagues had taken.

"Everything is done, but Mapako summons you elders to where he is, where the deceased is, immediately. He will tell you more when you get there."

"It's not about the rat? Mapako is behaving like a kid now." Mukoko looked questioningly at the men. Murehwa had died at the age of sixty, without having married. He had lived alone at his small compound of two huts. Villagers knew him as a *tsvimborume*, who never even lured the village prostitute to his hut because the female goblin he lived with would not tolerate females at the homestead. Mukoko assumed Mapako wanted to talk about the issue of the rat. It was the custom to bury a rat with a bachelor.

"He did not tell you why he wants us?" Mukoko rose, but he sat down quickly again.

"Mapako is like that... he is always hesitant about what he does," the elder with a long pipe and scruffy beard complained, rising from his seat. He sunk his head in the collar of his big overcoat. He was loath to leave the fireplace. "The burial is this afternoon and he is behaving as if we have the whole day to ourselves." The eyes of Mapako's colleagues urged the elders to rise and accompany them.

"Soon the gravediggers will be sending word that they are finished with the grave; let us go and hear what he has to say." Mukoko rose to encourage the others to follow him. Three elders behind him, Mukoko grumbled his way to the hut where the deceased lay. They filed into the hut that was surrounded by mournful women singing. The women discerned that something was amiss by the look on the elders' faces. What could it be? The question hung on their faces and speculation began to rear its ugly head.

"It must be the goblin," a woman whispered to a friend when the elders closed the door behind them.

"He is to be buried with it," concluded another of the women. "Who will touch such things?" She drew back as if her friend was the goblin.

Inside the hut Mukoko and the elders sat on the *chigaramakumucha* mud bench with the hunched Mapako, but anxiety did not allow them to settle properly. They looked around and shifted on the bench, casting suspicious glances at the open coffin. The lid of the coffin lay on the floor.

"Mhofu, I have summoned you to help me," Mapako addressed the elder with the long pipe. "I noticed... that the manhood of the deceased is erect." Mapako looked at them beseechingly, appearing awash with fear. He must have been frightened like a rat when he remained alone with the deceased.

"Ah, you mean the penis is . . .?" Mhofu did not finish his question. He relieved his mouth of the long pipe and put it in the pocket of his overcoat. They all heard what Mapako was trying to say, but the elders could not believe it. They shook their heads slowly in amazement. They could not say a word. Mukoko shifted to the front of the bench. He was the one nearest to the coffin.

"You can see for yourself," he said, as he pointed at the coffin, which lay at the far end of the hut opposite the door.

"Show us." Mukoko leaned forward but did not move towards the coffin. Mapako leapt from where he sat and removed the blanket covering the deceased and pulled the shroud up from the legs to the waist. The old men rose to get a full view of the body. The member in question pointed upwards, rigid as if ready for a sexual encounter. For a moment the elders remained motionless, letting out shocked exclamations.

Mukoko was the first to go back to his seat, followed by the scruffy bearded elder who cupped his mouth as if his teeth were threatening to fall out. The other two elders remained on their feet, eyeing the door as if they wanted to leave, until Mukoko told them to sit down. Mapako slowly returned the shroud to its former position, with reverence, unlike the manner in which he had pulled it up. He performed this action as if the deceased had complained about his earlier disrespect. The elders sat wrapped in thought, their faces to the ground. They were taut and defensive, except for Mapako who braved the repressive mood in the hut to ask, "Is it not desirable that we consult the spirit mediums?"

"I have never heard of such a thing." The long pipe was in the mouth again but it was not lit, despite the situation demanding that he smoke.

"Me neither." The elder's voice was thin and loud. He was about to disown his nephew.

"The man was too ill to entertain thoughts of sex. I came to see him the day before yesterday. He could not talk or eat," Mukoko recalled, shaking his head vigorously. They all agreed that such a thing never happened. It was taboo for an erection to take place when a person was dead. "In the meantime we will send word to the headman who will inform the chief about this." He did not specify what 'this' was. What could he say?

"I hope you will now release me because I have finished my task," Mapako said in a demanding voice. He rose and stood at the door holding the wooden latch.

"How can you say that? Anyway, you are still required here. I will remain in here with Mhofu. When the time comes you will be asked to accompany Chizema to the headman. We will consult the spirit mediums, but before we do that all the relatives of the deceased should be called for an impromptu meeting to discuss this issue." Mukoko was the eldest of all the elders. He was an old man who never compromised the traditions and customs of the village. His bald head shone above a frail stooping frame. His thin walking stick shone with oil from his glistening palms.

The women stopped singing when they felt that the elders had been taking too long inside the hut. The drummer left the drum lying on its side to hear what gossip was circulating among the other mourners. Before the chief was informed, Mukoko and the other village elders consulted relatives of the deceased. Word soon enveloped the village about the deceased's condition, creating a lot of excitement. With speed, the unfortunate condition of the deceased was whispered beyond the village and the news drew so much interest in the surrounding villages that people stormed to the funeral compound with inquisitive minds. Their faces seemed to demand to be shown the erection. The tale about the female goblin was the favoured explanation for the deceased's condition. Murehwa died during the act, they said. The female goblin could stimulate even the dead to bring about an erection. Goblins are dead people used by witches to extract blood and, in the case of Murehwa, to extract semen for witchcraft purposes. Some even suggested that extraction was at that very time taking place. It was unfortunate that the naked eye could not see what was happening. A spirit medium could extricate Murehwa from the goblin. There were female and male goblins and their task was almost the same. Suppositions and fantasies floated from people's mouths.

But before Mapako and Chizema left for the headman's court, Matope, the family *sahwira*, approached Chikweshe, the other surviving brother of the dead man's father.

"Before we start running around naked, let me do my part, which I think will appease the spirit of our dead nephew." Matope pulled Chikweshe away from the curious listeners, who crowded around the uncle every time he appeared alone. The *sahwira*'s whispering made the menfolk feel curious and uncomfortable.

"I am not thinking of cutting the mischievous penis." Matope laughed a dry laugh that did not amuse Chikweshe, who seemed to have avoided bathing that morning. Although he had a clean-shaven face, Chikweshe's skin was as if no petroleum jelly had ever been rubbed on it in his many years of existence. He wore a navy blue pinstriped suit that had been mended with assorted patches by an unprofessional hand. "The *sahwira* act that I hope will disturb the erection can only be carried out by singing women. The women must not wear pants underneath their petticoats and dresses. They should dance around the deceased and taunt him, bombard him with vulgarism, sweet talk him to rest in peace." Matope did not pull any punches and observed the impact of his plan upon Chikweshe.

Chikweshe smiled a little, a smile that was immediately consumed by the anxiety greying his face. "I like the idea of taunting the dead or straight talking them, like we do with the shadow of a deceased during a wake."

"That is the idea, Chikweshe," Matope was quick to agree with him, in a loud voice that drew the attention of the curious mourners.

"But . . . but these women with no pants dancing around the dead? The dead must be respected Matope . . . no knickers! The elders will never allow such a thing to take place."

"Such things are not made public. I will ask my wife, who is also your *sahwira*, to do the performance. She will instruct our daughter and daughters-in-law to join her in the dance. She will do the talking, backed by the singing of my daughter and daughters-in-law."

"You mean your daughters-in-law will agree to dance without . . . ?" Chikweshe could not believe Matope, considering their religious beliefs. He squeezed his lips between his thumb and forefinger.

"I am not forcing anyone, but what I know is that *sahwiras* do all the dirty work for their friends. This *sahwira* relationship is a crucial thing. I know my wife and daughter are aware of the seriousness of their duties."

"I do not know . . . you'd better ask the elders." His voice trailed behind Matope, who was already approaching Mukoko who stood talking to a group of men behind the hut in which the deceased lay.

Matope did not take long talking with Mukoko, who agreed to the dancing as long as it was done with the authorization of the uncle of the deceased. Matope did not mention that the women would dance with no pants. He just said the women would follow the customary duty of taunting the deceased when complications arose, such as when the deceased emitted a horrible smell, failed to fit in the coffin or cast a shadow for unclear reasons. The *sahwira*'s duty was to talk to the dead and persuade him or her to 'behave', as in the case of Murehwa. The deceased could be scolded for embarrassing the surviving family.

In no time Matope, with his troupe of performers – his wife, daughter and two daughters-in-law, entered the hut where the deceased lay. A few other women also sneaked into the hut when Matope's wife and daughters entered. Mukoko and the elders did not think that Matope's act required their presence so they excused themselves and remained by the fire, anxiously awaiting the result. Chikweshe and another relative were present for the *sahwira* act. They sat on the mud bench and conversed in very low voices, while the women sat on the floor opposite the bench. The coffin lid covered the lower part of the body, exposing the head and chest of the deceased.

"Chikweshe, your son Murehwa lies here dead. Although advanced in age he did not marry and he has no seed. It saddens us greatly as the *sahwira*. I am joined with my family to bid him farewell. But I would very much like to know the cause of his death." Matope's wife started to sing words to a well-known *jit* tune; the other women in the hut joined in with a variety of voices, the words being improvised to suit the situation. Matope's wife narrated the life of the deceased in song, a life that had been miserable because he never confided in anyone, male or female. "Murehwa never had a love relationship. He was a loner. No woman in the village would claim him dead or alive. He lived his own life using his axe to carve stylish hoe handles. He moved around with his adze." Matope's wife and daughter shook their bodies in a vigorous dance with their backs to the coffin. They bent forward and swung their behinds to the left and to the right above the coffin. Matope's wife laughed seductively, "Murehwa, here is that of which you did not partake, that which you did not take pleasure in." Accompanied by her daughter she hopped backwards towards the coffin, her buttocks raised like those of a peacock. "Murehwa, here is that of which you did not partake, do not hold a grudge against us or your relatives, you should have asked and I would have done something about . . ."

She continued scornfully, "Surely there were women who were prepared to come to your bed if only you had had the courage to approach us, we of the dresses. Certainly." Bent forwards, she again skipped backwards, swinging her behind from side to side near the coffin. The other women clapped their hands and sang without paying much attention to what the *sahwira*'s wife was saying. Matope's daughters-in-law danced but kept their distance from the coffin.

Outside the hut the drummer joined in, beating his drum accompanied by the multitude of singing mourners. The door was opened and the elders, from where they sat, watched the young men dancing to the *jit* tune. The *sahwira* act had spread throughout the whole funeral compound. Mourners enjoyed themselves and grief was temporarily forsaken. They suspected that the *sahwira* was appeasing the spirit of Murehwa in song and dance, but, besides Chikweshe, no one else knew that the dancers inside the hut were knicker-less during the hopping and skipping act. It was a long, one song performance in which most people in the village took part.

At the end of the song, people were asked to leave the hut. Matope and Chikweshe remained to examine the effect of the *sahwira* performance on the deceased. The creaky door was closed. Chikweshe was hesitant, doubting that the act had produced the desired result. The song had taken too long for his patience. Matope lifted the coffin lid and carefully removed the blanket and shroud to expose Murehwa's penis. It had shrunk like a worm whose insides had been squeezed out. They looked at each other and Chikweshe smiled, shaking his head slowly as he walked to the bench. There was a knock at the door and old Mukoko announced in his frail voice, "The men from the graveyard say they have finished preparing the grave." His voice was forlorn.

Matope opened the door to let Mukoko in. He was alone, but the anxious eyes of the mourners followed his every step. Matope led Mukoko to the coffin and stretched his open hands before the coffin to indicate the favourable outcome. Old Mukoko nodded and gestured that Matope should cover the body and close the coffin.

Relieved, he asked, "Have the people been fed?"

Why My Love

I watched a bee settle
on a flower.
It caressed the petals,
the hind legs
resting on soft sepals.
I saw it dip its
long lip into the pistil
with passion
and buzz away.

In no time
another bee came,
buzzed with persuasion
around the same flower,
touched fondly the yielding
sepals,

kissed with
affection the petals
and buzzed away.

In disgust
my voice trembled
why my love, why . . .?

You Know What I Mean

She is a lass
upmarket
you know what I mean
a woman of class
connected
you know what I mean
fast life lady
a babe
you know what I mean
a you know what I mean wench
you know what I mean.

JOHN EPPEL

JOHN EFFEL

Malnourished Sonnet

The unburnt pot
on my desk
could never carry water
from the Umzingwane Dam,
or beer brewed
in a forty gallon drum,
or the spirit
of a stillborn baby;

but it is a useful receptacle
for my pen,
screwdriver,
tweezers,
nail clippers,
and Ingrid Jonker medal.

Afrika

"Do you think, by spelling it with a 'k',
that you will make it ... well ... more African?
that calling it Robert Mugabe Way
instead of Grey Street (what's in a man?)
the vendors squatting underneath the sign
will somehow earn more money down the line?"

"Look, friend, sacrifices have to be made ...
I lost a favourite uncle in the war,
my post-doctoral thesis was delayed,
I'm still ... well ... relatively speaking, poor.
Rome – it's your round – wasn't built in a day ...
let's make a start ... let's spell it with a 'k'."

The Debate

The discussions on a government of national unity (in a country near you) had become fatally deadlocked. The mediator, an eminent African (name supplied), came up with an idea, inspired by the recent Presidential debates in the USA, which, he believed, would result in a settlement.

First he had to relocate the three antagonists and frog-march them, if necessary, back to the negotiating table. Mr Wynken was at home with his family, tucking into a copious supply of *Kentucky Fried Chicken* with chips, tomato sauce, and lashings of *Coca-Cola*. They were in the lounge watching a re-run of the American soap, *Dallas*. Professor Blynken was visiting at one of his 'small houses', a Tuscan-style mansion with columns made of asbestos sewage pipes, in the City of Kings, Bulawayo. Comrade Nod, with an entourage of sixty family members, cronies, and security guards, was spending the weekend at a luxury hotel in Mauritius.

At last, the antagonists were reassembled at the table, the one made out of Rhodesian teak railway sleepers, and the mediator made this proposition: "Boys, let's settle it with a debate! You know, like McCain and Whatsisname! With the Americans, as with you people, the economy is the central issue, so let's have a debate, on TV, boys, and let the electorate decide who gives the most convincing argument on restoring your economy. The winner will be allowed to dish out cabinet posts, including the newly established one, and most coveted, of Minister of Rural Beauty Pageants." The three antagonists licked their lips a few times and then decided to go for it.

The people were duly informed of the live debate and its purposes. Each of the antagonists would have five minutes to explain his plan to revive the economy. The winner would be decided by the loudness of applause of an invited audience: a hundred citizens randomly selected from the general populace.

The cameras rolled and the debate began. The mediator played the host. Mr Wynken elected to speak first. "When the paper runs out, all transactions should be carried out in this country's most stable commodity: empties. I propose a currency of coke and *Fanta* bottles in the soft drinks line, and wine and beer bottles in the hard drinks line. The *scud*, as long as it is carefully rinsed, could also be included." He went on to give numerical values to the various types and colours of bottles, so, for example, green beer bottles would be more valuable than brown beer bottles; and family size coke and *Fanta* bottles would be more valuable than those of standard size. Professor Blynken pointed out that *scuds*, by any other name, could not be construed as bottles. Comrade Nod said that, in any case, Mr Wynken was too ugly to be a serious contender.

After the applause died down, the next speaker commenced. It was Professor Blynken. "What I propose is a logical extension of the current system. Let anyone who has access to a photocopier and A4 bond paper, copy however much money he needs for that day's expenses. To be fair to the majority who do not have access to modern technology, lower denominations may be traced or even sketched on any surface that will carry the image: flat stones, pieces of wood, even banana peels." Mr Wynken undermined the argument by jokingly suggesting underwear, and Comrade Nod wondered if Professor Blynken wasn't too intelligent to be a serious contender. Professor Blynken received about the same volume of applause as Mr Wynken.

Finally, it was Comrade Nod's turn. "The West still negates our sovereignties by way of control of our resources, in the process making us mere chattels in our own lands, mere minders of its transnational interests. In my own country and other sister states in Southern Africa, the most visible form of this control has been over land despoiled from us at the onset of British colonialism.

"That control largely persists, although it stands firmly challenged in my country, thereby triggering the current stand-off between us and Britain, supported by her cousin states, most notably the United States and Australia. Mr Humpty, Mr Dumpty and now Mr Skippy's sense of human rights precludes our people's right to their God-given resources, which in their view must be controlled by their kith and kin. I am termed dictator because I have rejected this supremacist view and frustrated the neo-colonialists.

"Let these sinister governments be told here and now that we will not allow a regime change authored by outsiders. Mr Humpty and Mr Dumpty have no role to play in our national affairs. They are mischievous outsiders and should therefore keep out! The colonial sun set a long time ago; in 1980 in the case of my dear country, and hence I . . . ooooooh . . . we will never be a colony again. Never!

"We do not deserve sanctions. We are patriots and we know how to deal with our problems. We have done so in the past, well before Humpty and Dumpty were known politically. We have our own regional and continental organizations and communities.

"Yes, for us post-colonials, we still have an aloof immigrant settler landed gentry, all-white, all-royal, all untouchable, all-western supported, pitted against a bitter, disinherited, landless, poverty-begrimed, right-less communal black majority we have vowed to empower . . . ooooooh . . . and in the cause of whom we continue to be vilified, in a country that is ours and very African and sovereign. Hence, in spite of the present global milieu of technological sophistication, we remain a modern world divided by old dichotomies and old asymmetries that make genuine calls for . . . er . . . digital solidarity sound hollow.

"Er . . . this gathering is a re-enactment in my view of that togetherness, the partnership, the co-operation that has seen processes taking place here leading to a number of our countries attaining their independence. Ooooooh! I said I will never ever attack an African leader in public, never ever! In our forum we will tell each other about what we think of each other. I will get my day!

"Yesterday as we of my country sought to liberate ourselves and the fight was between us, the people of my country, and the oppressors, it was the Front Line States who together with us shaped the struggle that led to our liberation and independence, therefore . . . er . . . *pamberi* the economy, *pasi* the drought, *pasi* sanctions, *pamberi* . . . er . . . me."

Comrade Nod received about the same volume of applause as Mr Wynken and Professor Blynken, so the stalemate continues. Cold comfort for the antagonists and the mediator was provided in the form of *Chivas Regal* on the rocks with a splash of *Fanta* orange.

The Coming of the Rains

Romantics like Rousseau talk nonsense
when they insist that we are born free,
though he's right about the chains. See,
you didn't know which side of the fence

you would end up attempting to climb.
You had no say in your spawning,
or the biology of your thing,
or your complexion. Yet time and time

again we are told of a free press,
a free state, free will, freedom of speech,
freedom to write what we like, to preach
what we like, freedom to make a mess.

"It's often safer to be in chains,"
says Franz Kafka, "than to be free."
But safety is not the issue, see –
it's the rains, the coming of the rains.

Ghostly Galleon

A ghostly galleon plies the seas
that give and take, build and break
on Africa's ex-colonies:
on Mozambique, Namibia,
(sometimes mild and sometimes wild),
Angola and South Africa.

Bang, bang, bang, the *An Yue Jiang*
is looking for a port,
but workers on the Durban docks
said, "Nothing of the sort!

"Take your AKs somewhere else,
your mortars and grenades;
they'll use those bullets on working folk,
boys with dreadlocks and girls with braids,
waiters, vendors, gardeners, maids,
labourers with picks and spades,
farmers dragging the oxen's yoke."

There is a ghostly galleon
that plies the southern seas;
it carries death for working folk:
cannons and RPGs.

It tried to dock in Durban
to drop its deadly load,
but the Durban Dockers' Union
upheld the workers' code.

Well it's a bang, bang, bang, the *An Yue Jiang*
Is sailing round the Cape
With toys for the Boys that make a loud noise,
that kill and maim and rape.

Salute the Durban Dockers
salute those workers bold:
they saved a thousand comrades
from misery untold.
They saved a thousand comrades,
but only for a day:
the ghostly galleon will be back –
terror is here to stay.

Democracy at Work and at Play

The Reverend Benate Jojova was thrilled that he would be playing an active role in Zimbabwe's constitution-making process. He had been invited to join an outreach programme in Gulati, not far from Bulawayo. Since he lived in Masvingo, and there were several outreach programmes in that district, he was a little puzzled as to why the organizers had decided to send him to Bulawayo, considering travel and accommodation expenses. Never mind. What an adventure! And what a feather in Zimbabwe's cap! It took the West... how long? – a thousand years to achieve democracy, and here we are, a little over thirty years old – our Lord's age on earth – poised to achieve government by the people, of the people... er... darn those English prepositions... to?... with?... over? Never mind.

His wife, Mai Queeny, had packed his suitcase with a spare dog collar and clothes for three days at the Heaven on Earth Guest House, where he would be boarding with four other outreach members, none of them, as it turned out, from Bulawayo, but all devout Christians. Their transport was an almost new *Nissan Hardbody* double cab, which had been seconded to the Select Committee of Parliament on the New Constitution (COPAC) by a Masvingo Member of Parliament. The United Nations was footing the bill so there were no unseemly arguments about the exorbitant rental.

They waited arm in arm outside the rectory, for their colleagues to arrive. Mai Queeny had made her husband a thermos flask of oxtail soup, and packed him some peanut butter sandwiches for the road. "Don't forget to take your pills," she reminded him, and then, jokingly, "beware of *izintombi*! You know the reputation those Bulawayo girls have!" She gave his arm a loving squeeze.

"*Nyarara*, woman!" Benate chuckled. "I'm an old man – of the cloth. My hanky panky days are well and truly over."

"Then why does your Bible always open on the 'Song of Solomon'?"

"Ah... 'Thy lips, O my spouse, drop as the honeycomb: honey and milk are under thy tongue; and the smell of thy garments is like the smell of Lebanon'. That's where Yvonne got the title of her novel."

"You and half the world are in love with Yvonne Vera. Now you are going to pay homage to her in the city she so loved. I am a little jealous, you know."

The Reverend Jojova regarded himself as something of an authority on Zimbabwean literature, in particular Yvonne Vera, who had been the subject of his Master's thesis: *Beautifying the Horror: Biblical Influences in the Writings of Yvonne Vera* According to him, the cross, with its associations of extreme violence and ineffable beauty, was the central trope of all her writings. "More than that, my dear, I'll be entering the physical world of her greatest novel, *The Stone Virgins*..."

"You leave those virgins alone, *inzwa*?"

They were both chuckling away when the transport arrived. Benate was the last passenger. His wife lifted his suitcase into the open back of the truck while he climbed into the last remaining space in the passenger seat. Greetings were made all round – these eminent persons of Masvingo knew each other – then farewells, and off they veered in the direction of Bulawayo. Apart from the multiple police road blocks (where smallish bills exchanged hands) it was a most pleasant journey. *Padkos* was shared as convivially as the conversation, which, naturally, focussed on the constitution-making process. All agreed that the current mutilated Lancaster House Constitution had to go, and there was some friendly dissent about the pros and cons of the Kariba draft, the NCA draft, and even the rejected Chidyausiku Constitution.

By the time they had located the Heaven on Earth Guest House in one of Bulawayo's leafier suburbs, the sun had dipped below the horizon, and the sky – how did Yvonne Vera put it? – that low you could lick it – full of dust and wood smoke (in the windy month of August) – was glowing orange. They were warmly welcomed by their gracious hostess, Inkosikazi 'Vuvuzela' Bhebe (her nickname derived from the fact that she delighted in sprinkling talcum powder on her carpets, and sometimes on her guests), and shown to their rooms: prettily thatched rondavels. After unpacking and washing, the outreach team were treated to a delicious supper of fried chicken and rice followed by Vuvuzela's speciality: *amasi* with fresh fruit. They retired early in order to be ready for the next day's trip to Tokwe School in Gulati communal lands. Before the power cut out, Benate read avidly, not from his Bible but from his dog-eared copy of *The Stone Virgins*. He was fascinated by the character, Sibaso, who could cavort with the body of a woman he had just decapitated and then, shortly after, rape and mutilate the sister, who must have witnessed the *danse macabre*. All that gore! One thing puzzled him, however: on page 61, the words: "A knee lifts up to touch the bottom of her legs." Was Sibaso a dwarf?

Perhaps because it was close to the National Park, perhaps because of its mountainous, bushy terrain, which would have made it difficult for the North Korean built armoured cars to traverse, the Fifth Brigade kept their Gulati incursions to a minimum. Dissidents, on the other hand, thrived there. Notorious killers like 'Fidel Castro', 'Idi Amin', 'Danger', and 'Gayigusu' regularly travelled through the region, wreaking havoc. Benate wondered if Sibaso wasn't based on one of these real life monsters. Just north-east of Gulati lay Adam's Farm, a Christian commune, where, at the behest of some local squatters (and who knows which Chef?) dissidents axed to death 16 people including women and children, and a baby.

The road (sometimes no more than a track) to Tokwe school was almost impassable in places. Thank goodness the *Nissan Hardbody* had four-wheel drive. Benate and the others were stunned by the beauty of the landscape, and imagined how easily fugitives could hide themselves in those lichen-spattered, cave-pocked granite hills. When they arrived at the venue they saw a gathering of about 200 locals, mainly elderly women and children. They were met by a contingent of uniformed police and half a dozen young and youngish men who claimed to be war veterans or war collaborators. The hairs stood up on the back of Benate's neck when he noticed that they were armed with branches and machetes.

The police spokesman welcomed the outreach team and wondered if any of them could speak Ndebele; if not one of the war veterans would translate for them. One of Benate's colleagues said they had been instructed to speak in English, and what the locals couldn't understand, Reverend Jojova would render in halting Ndebele. The team's driver, a retired headmaster, would chair the meeting while the others observed and took notes. He rummaged in the back of the truck and brought out a loud hailer. He switched it on, tested it, turned to the assembled crowd and addressed them: "*Salibonani abantumnyama!*"

"*Yebo!*" from about a dozen voices.

"*Linjani?*"

"*Siyaphila!*" from about half a dozen voices.

Then he proceeded in English – to introduce the outreach members and to explain their mission. "As a country of democratic principles, Zimbabwe wants to create a people-driven constitution, which protects the rights of every individual –"

"What about homosexuals?" interrupted one of the war vets.

One of the few men in the crowd put up his hand. "Er ... yes?"

"Homosexuals should be stoned to death in public." This received an enthusiastic response from the crowd. Some women began to ululate.

The retired headmaster shouted into his loud hailer: "Please may we leave questions and answers until I have completed my address?" Two hours later his address was completed. He then asked what the crowd in general expected from a constitution, which would be the supreme law of the land and would shape Zimbabwe's destiny.

An ancient woman put up her hand. "We want a king." Cheers and ululations.

Another hand went up; a very old woman. "Our youth must be more respectful. They should greet us properly. The girls must go down on their knees."

Benate and the others were busy making notes. The policemen stood by smiling while the war vets moved in among the crowds, tapping their weapons against their thighs. A third hand went up; an old woman. She spoke in the vernacular: "There should be a minimum age limit on when children could be raped. It is my request that in the new constitution girls should not be raped before they are 24 years."

An old man wearing a straw hat put up his hand. "We want strong laws that will ban women from wearing trousers. How can I propose to her if she looks like a man? Do you think I am a homosexual like Blair?" Applause and loud laughter.

"Yes," shouted another old man, "and mini-skirts should also be banned. These girls are asking to be 'rapped'."

A slightly younger woman: "Our girls must be stopped from going to Kezi Business Centre where they are becoming prostitutes."

"There should be more stories like 'Superman' on the wireless."

"Clinics should be free like in Rhodesia."

It went on like this until Benate stood up and asked them if they would be less er... personal for a while, and look at issues like devolution, the electorate, parliament etc. The first speaker, the one who had denounced homosexuals, put up his hand – he seemed to be in cahoots with the war veterans – "We should have a president for life." Stunned silence.

One of the war vets strutted up to the retired headmaster, jerked the loud hailer from his hand, and addressed the now restive crowd. "Those of you who disagree with a life president must point out your houses to me." He felt in his trousers pocket and brought out a box of matches. He shook the box. "Let us have a show of hands." Dead silence. No hands went up. The policemen stood by smiling. The war vet threw the loud hailer to the ground and turned to the outreach team, who were all on their feet. "You sell outs!" he snarled, "crawl back to your MDC masters in Masvingo and tell them we already have a constitution – it's called the Kariba Draft. Go, before I set your truck alight!"

With ashen faces the five important persons, all somewhat overweight, scrambled for their vehicle and drove away. When Benate looked back he saw the war vets climbing into the rear of the police *bakkie*, waving their branches and their machetes in triumph. They drove back to Bulawayo in dead silence.

Their woes were not over. They found their suitcases strewn outside the gates of the Heaven on Earth guest house. After ten minutes of hooting and ringing the bell, they heard the side gate opening, and there stood Mrs Bhebe, arms akimbo, a furious expression on her face. "Your sponsors are refusing to pay me. Go before I set my dogs on you."

"We have a democratic right –"

"Go!"

The portly, middle-aged five, scrambled for their suitcases, piled them into the back of the truck, squeezed into the cab, and veered off in the direction of Masvingo. Fortunately there was enough money left to fill the tank of the MP's truck.

Back at the rectory, while dunking a rusk into strong, milky tea, Benate was soothed with words and fingers by the solicitous Queeny, who hinted of even better things to come, later, in their bedroom.

After the actualisation of Queeny's hints, while she slept, Benate lit a candle, and began to read – not his Bible but *The Stone Virgins*, and when he got to the sentence on page 69: 'He throws her towards himself", he muttered, "Darn these English prepositions"; but then his postmodern training kicked in and his face broke into a broad smile. He wished Queeny were awake so that he could proclaim his insight. Of course! This is subversive writing. Yvonne is insinuating the alterity of the subaltern into governing epistemes, granting it textual amplitude. Indeed, she manifests a semiotic modality, which unsettles the Colonialist as well as the Nationalist space. It's time for me to do my PhD, and my working title . . . my working title . . . let's see . . . er . . . how about: *Democracy at Work and at Play: The Subversive Function of Faulty Grammar and Mixed Metaphors in the Writings of Yvonne Vera.*

The Reverend Benate Jojova MA, smiled happily, closed his book, blew out the candle, snuggled against the warm expansive body of his good wife, and fell into a deep, untroubled sleep.

Day and Night

A punctuation of crows slows down the syntax of the sky;
paragraphs billow like reader-friendly clouds, easy on the eye.
Pointing towards Johannesburg, a fading vapour trail
suggests either a cliffhanger or a sting in the tail.
The sun at noon, about to fall, is the peripeteia
which fills the reader with forebodings of pity and fear.
This sky is masculine, a palimpsest; the Holy Mother,
almost completely erased, has become the wholly other.

Now the sun is setting, exclamation marks appear like trees;
listen to the onomatopoeia of a gentle breeze;
feel its sibilance cool against your cheeks; then, one by one,
the stars appear like poems not yet written, poems long gone.
The rising moon is orange first, then gold, then lemon yellow;
It feels like aloe vera slime, sounds like a violoncello.
This is now a female sky, a palimpsest; the Mighty Lord,
almost completely erased, has become a flighty bawd.

The CWM

Somalia has its warlords, Zimbabwe has its CWMs or cheeky white madams. When governance breaks down, anarchy looms, and nations revert to tribes, some dominant, many subordinate. In Zimbabwe one dominant tribe happens to be elderly white women who, since that cruciferous plant, woad, with which the ancient Britons stained their bodies, is unavailable in Zimbabwe, use a preparation known as blue rinse. Because they cover themselves from head to foot in a crease-resistant synthetic fabric called crimplene, it is not possible to determine the extent to which they stain their bodies in the manner of their warlike ancestors, but they certainly stain their naturally grey, silver or white topknots – to the approximate shade of methylated spirit.

Our neighbourhood had been, over the past ten years, declining not unpleasantly into anarchy. We all had at least one illegal rooster on our premises; dogs had metamorphosed from recognizable breeds like labradors and German shepherds to skinny, whippet-like creatures that could survive on grass, known, euphemistically (and anachronistically), as Grey Street terriers; cats had become feral, and lived in storm drains or on the roofs of houses; quacking Aylesburys had been exterminated by hissing Muscovies; nuclear families of four or five had been squeezed out by extended families and their lodgers of twelve or twenty.

Nobody complained when we had noisy parties, which went on all night and well into the next day; or when we built huge, threatening bonfires; or when we felled trees; or when we extended our houses using building materials that even the most tolerant of city councils would condemn. Nobody complained when our roosters began issuing challenges at one another, continually, from midnight onwards; or when our dogs yapped for hours at the moon; or when our children communicated over crumbling walls at the tops of their pre-pubertal voices. Then Mrs MacSnatch moved in, and all changed, changed utterly.

To continue in the words of the immortal bard, a terrible beauty was born (or, should I say, re-born?), the terrible beauty of civilised behaviour according to the predilections of half a dozen cheeky white madams. Our properties are large, mostly over an acre in extent, and one of these properties was converted into a cluster of upmarket houses, six in all, occupied by influential members of the CWM tribe. We watched the complex grow over a period of about six months, not that we could see much once the two metre brick wall topped with razor wire and an electrified fence had gone up. The occupants we learned, via the reliable domestic worker circuit, were widows of commercial farmers, businessmen, and white collar criminals who had died of unrequited rugby. The youngest was 70, the oldest, 93; all wore crimplene slacks or frocks ranging in colour from mustard to chilli pepper; all had blow-waved blue hair with matching ramified blood vessels. Mrs MacSnatch was their acknowledged legislator.

She began with the roosters (she called them cocks). Each one of us got the dreaded phone call: "Hullo, my name is Valery MacSnatch. I live just down the road from you, and your cock is driving me crazy. I'm not a well person, you know, and I require a good night's sleep. No sooner have I shut my eyes of a night, than your cock starts its nonsense. I have informed the City Council, and if you don't do something about that creature immediately, they will be paying you a visit. I have also informed the police. Please, I expect good neighbourliness from you people." I had been keeping chickens for more than 20 years. This was the first time anyone had ever complained. She had moved into the cluster complex from her palatial Burnside residence a fortnight before.

Then it was the cats (she called them pussies). "Can't you keep your pussies where they belong, instead of letting them roam the gutters and the roof tops? Yowling like banshees! Pussies like to be stroked, to be rubbed, to be scratched, in short, to be pampered. They do not deserve this neglect. Well, I tell you, and I tell you straight, my friend, the S.P.C.A. will know about this.

Mrs Ridgeback is a close friend of mine, and she does not tolerate, I repeat, not tolerate, pet neglect. Honestly, you people!"

Then it was the dogs (bow-wows), and then the children (brats), and then the music (noise), and so on, until our neighbourhood became as quiet as a mausoleum, and as sombre. When the cheeky white madam glides by in her 1956 *Humber Super Snipe*, on her way to sip tea and nibble ginger snaps with another of her tribe, I breathe a sigh of relief and turn up the volume – a little – on my new Chiwoniso CD.

Broke-Buttock Blues

They beat me with branches wrapped up in barb-wire,
they beat me with branches wrapped up in barb-wire;
my baby she crying, her face is on fire.

They say you are sell-out, you vote Tsvangirai,
they say you are sell-out, you vote Tsvangirai;
my baby, she dying, please God, tell me why?

They beat first my head then my back then my bums,
they beat first my head then my back then my bums;
they laugh and they say is like playing the drums.

I beg them for water, they say go ask Blair,
I beg them for water, they say go ask Blair.
Please, put out the fire in Mucheche's hair?

My bottom is broken, can not sit or stand,
my bottom is broken, can not sit or stand;
Mucheche can't breathe with her mouth in the sand.

They burned all our mealies, our chickens, our dog,
they burned all our mealies, our chickens, our dog;
my uncle, they hit him to death with a log.

For hours they beat me, for hours I cry,
for hours they beat me, for hours I cry;
please God, save my baby, do not let her die?

When they leave, like a tortoise I crawl very slow,
when they leave, like a tortoise I crawl very slow;
but my baby stopped crying a long time ago,
mwana wangu stopped crying a long time ago.

Discarded

The University of Lupane is a stretch of open field. It was here in the month of May, 2008, that ZANU-PF officials held a *pungwe* presided over by Senior Assistant Commissioner Happyboy Gava. He told the exhausted villagers that, according to the constitution, only a war veteran could be made president of 'our sovereign nation'. Whenever he used the word 'sovereign' he dabbed his plump cheeks – all that pork roast – with a white hanky, in the style of Kenneth Kaunda.

Attending the meeting was ardent ZANU-PF supporter, Willibald Nyoni. At 30 years old he was the proud possessor of 20 hectares of land, part of a white 'owned' farm, which the Third *Chimurenga* had restored to the indigenous peoples of Zimbabwe. For three months Willibald had lived like a king: meat, beer and girls; day after day, night after night. Then the firewood ran out; suddenly Willibald was destitute: no meat, no beer, no girls. For the second time in his life, Willibald was rescued by the government. They offered to feed him and perhaps even pay him for services rendered, in short, to help the war vets and the militias terrorize opposition supporters.

"Never again will we be a colony!" shouted the Senior Assistant Commissioner. (It seemed that the higher echelons of government shared the same speech writer.) "We are a sovereign entity." Dab of hanky. "Let Brown and Bush beware! Let that homosexual across the border beware! Let puppet sanctions-mongers beware! We are of the fist!" At this point he incongruously waved his hanky. "If we do not win the run-off, there will be conflict in our sovereign land [dab, dab]: black against black. You must defend the revolution; otherwise we will go back to the bush and fight." He was sweating profusely even though there was a chill southeaster blowing from Johannesburg. His belly was so huge – he found pork crackling irresistible – that he had to wear his belt around his bum.

"Democracy is only for the educated. There is no day on which this sovereign [dab, dab] country will be handed over on a silver platter. How can we give power to those who have no knowledge of governance and no support from you, the local voters, but has (sic) support from puppets and homosexuals?" He went on in this manner for hours.

The next speaker was a war veteran (much too young to have fought in the Second *Chimurenga*) called Comrade Hotstuff. He was armed with an AK-47, which became an improvised guitar in a dance routine that combined *toyi-toyi* and *kwasa-kwasa*. When he began to speak, the rifle was restored to its original purpose, and he discharged a few rounds into the air – to revive audience attention. "Be warned: the soldiers are watching to see the polling station returns. *Pasi ne* Tsvangirai!"

"*Pasi.*"

"For every MDC vote in this constituency one of you will be shot dead. *Pasi ne* Brown!"

"*Pasi.*"

"Remember *Gukurahundi*! We have lists of MDC supporters. We know who you are! *Pasi ne* Bush!"

"*Pasi.*"

"If you want to die, if you want to have your homesteads burnt down, go ahead and vote for that puppet of the west, Tsvangirai! *Pamberi ne* Mugabe!"

"*Pamberi.*"

"*Pamberi ne* sovereignty!"

"*Pamberi.*"

"*Pamberi ne* Operation Vote Wisely!"

"*Pamberi.*"

Comrade Hotstuff then called upon voters to surrender their MDC cards and T-shirts, and gradually a small pile of these items grew at the size thirteen boots of the war vet. A youth wearing a ZANU-PF T-shirt arrived with a tin of paraffin and a box of matches – and the pile was soon blazing merrily.

Willibald Nyoni was assigned to a group of militias from Mashonaland who had recently been deployed to the region.

Their brief was to intimidate the rural folk into voting 'wisely'. Since he was native to that area, Willibald was given the task of providing the militia with meat, beer, and girls. This he did with commitment and enthusiasm. His greatest achievement, which earned him high praise, not only from the militias but from none other than Comrade Hotstuff, who partook of the subsequent spoils, was to commandeer an ox from the kraal of a successful re-settled farmer, indeed a neighbour and distant relative, Ndabazinhle Nyoni. Single-handedly Willibald drove the ox to the abandoned primary school where the militias had set up a torture centre, slaughtered it, gutted it, and skinned it. Then he chopped it into workable pieces and shared it out. Single-handedly he rounded up willing (i.e. hungry) girls, and a forty gallon drum full of opaque beer. What a feasting was there that night, what hanky-panky, well into the next day! Willibald Nyoni became a hero of the Struggle. *Aluta continua.*

The strategy set up by Joint Operations Command worked: His Excellency R.G. Mugabe was voted, unopposed, back into the driving seat, so to speak. Now loyalists like Willibald, who had done the dirty work for the Party, were no longer required; indeed they had become an embarrassment. What was Willibald's surprise when, a few days after the presidential run-off, three policemen armed with batons arrived at his plot and arrested him for stock theft? In court he admitted he had taken the ox as part of the continuing struggle. He was providing for patriots who were defending his beloved country from the evil machinations of the west. The magistrate, without once looking up, sentenced Willibald, without right of appeal, to nine years in jail, a veritable death sentence.

Song for WOZA

Women of this land arise,
fling your windows open wide,
let the breeze of change, denied,
let it take you by surprise.
Amandla omama!

Let it take you to the streets,
walk for freedom, walk for peace,
disarm with charm the armed police,
give them flowers and home-made treats.
Amandla abafazi!

Let it blow through corridors
where men of power strap their boots,
sip hot liquor, smoke cheroots,
boast of virgins and of whores.
Amandla amankazana!

Let it, when you go to jail,
keep your foreheads cool, your hearts,
keep refreshed the gentler arts –
then let it grow into a gale.
Amandla isifazana!

Soap Rhymes With Hope

Evening cestrum comes to mind: honey about to ferment,
to become mead, an intoxicating brew; bauhinia
comes to mind, synchronising its perfume with the rotation
of my bicycle wheels, on my way to teach willing children
that nothing in nature dies, that process is a conversion
of one form of energy into another, that tinder
turns to fire, thence to ashes, thence to a sweetener of soil.

Once, when I went down to Kew in late spring, the scent of lilacs
made me weep for home, for the syringa blossom that transformed
September to a drift of skirts eddying, pony tails
swishing. But winter's best fragrance was the sage leaf buddleia
that prospered in our neighbour's garden; and summer's was
                                            plumeria,
its common name suggested by a famous scent invented
centuries ago by perfumer, Muzio Frangipane.

Now, the mounds of household rubbish dumped along our public
                                            ways,
on verges, in storm drains, rivers, ponds, or set alight to stink –
a toxic, nauseating horror that rises not like incense
but settles for the nostrils of the devil. Now our houses
reek of 'war vets" armpits and other effects of soaplessness:
poverty, anxiety, trepidation, even terror:
a ferment that manufactures, not bubbles, but hopelessness.

The Big Five

It was at Punda Maria where, despite the intrusive mopane trees and the irritating call of the Cape turtle dove, we got our first sighting. We couldn't believe our good luck. If it wasn't for a herd of impalas leaping idiotically over the road, we might have been able, with our fancy camera, to play with its shadow, its reflection, its profile. You guessed it: a silver *Toyota Land Cruiser Prado VX Turbo Diesel*. My hand was shaking when I ticked it on the checklist.

Our two-night stay at the Punda Maria rest camp was all but ruined by the crowds of long-tail cassias, Natal mahoganies, sycamore figs, tamboties, and the ubiquitous mopane. The birds were intolerable, especially that raucous francolin! Even worse, a pack of hyenas insisted on patrolling the boundary fence. But all was not lost, for, parked two tents down from our campsite, was a *Range Rover*, 3.6 litre, V8 turbo-charged and intercooled diesel engine, glovebox illumination... smell those leather seats... and emblazoned on its rump, the proud words: 'Don't try to follow me – you won't make it'. We must have photographed it a hundred times.

After Punda Maria we headed south, in our 1978 *Datsun* with its faded yellow Zimbabwe number plate, towards Shingwedzi and, with the aid of our binoculars, we almost completed our checklist: *Mazda, Isuzu, Volkswagen, Ford, BMW, Honda, Opel, Nissan, Hyundai*... you name it. But we were obsessed with the Big Five, and we'd already been fortunate enough to encounter two of them. The famed Kanniedood Drive was a big disappointment because the bush was teeming with game: obnoxious giraffe, silly wildebeest, vain zebra, supercilious kudu... Even the skies were polluted, with kingfishers, bee eaters, storks, herons and, worst of all, eagles and vultures. At the sight of a ground hornbill waddling along the road with no fewer than three frogs in its repulsive beak, we almost decided to turn around and head for home.

If anything, our camping experience at Shingwedzi was even worse than those disturbed nights in Punda Maria. We had to erect our tent right under an apple leaf tree! The resident birds, none more obnoxious than the glossy starlings and the woodland kingfishers, completely spoiled our sundowner time; and our sleep was disturbed by the yelping of jackals and the eructations of rutting impala. We even had to listen to a leopard coughing. But then peace at last, nay joy, when we heard the arrival of the 'best 4x4 by far', the *Landrover Defender 2.5 TDi* with Aircon, CD-Radio, Power Steering, Centre Diff Lock/Rear Diff Lock, Customised Safari Equipment. Using our flash, we got in some good shots: from the back, from the front, and from both sides. We managed to get a wonderful close-up of the left back passenger door handle, a picture we intend to frame.

On our way to Balule we were surprised to find that the low-level causeway over the Olifants was under water. We, along with a number of other visitors, were afraid to attempt a crossing in case the powerful current swept us into the disgusting brown river. It seemed as if we had been marooned there for ages, pulling faces at the wire-tailed swallows and the yellow-billed storks, bored stupid by a fight between two male hippos, sickened by the cry of the fish eagle... when a seeming miracle took place. We heard the powerful diesel engine before we witnessed it: a snow white *Toyota Fortuner 3.0TD* 4x4 with all the mod cons including mp3, Elec. Windows, and Airbags. Almost simultaneously a huge rogue elephant with tusks that ploughed the earth before it, began crossing the causeway from the other side. There is no stopping one of the Big Five, however – except briefly, to engage low gear – and the *Fortuner* eased on to the causeway. The current swirled about its massive, beautifully treaded wheels as it approached the elephant, now flapping its ears like carpets being dusted. We began to giggle with excited apprehension. Predictably the elephant chickened out and backed away, allowing the *Fortuner* to cross over to glory. We cheered and cheered, as did the other stranded visitors, all deeply satisfied with our photos of that ineffable vehicle.

After an hour or two the water subsided sufficiently for us to attempt a crossing, and we were mightily relieved to get to the other side. Balule was a most rewarding camp site since we counted no fewer than thirteen white and silver *Toyota Hilux* Double Cabs within the boundary fence. If there were a sixth Big One, this vehicle would be It. Our disappointments were restricted to a few squirrels and an ugly pair of plum-coloured starlings. Oh, and the far too many Terminalia prunioides with their creamy flowers in slender axillary spikes, their purplish red fruits, and their long, drooping branches.

The next day turned out to be our last because we got to see the last of the Big Five; consequently there was no longer any point in enduring unpleasant scenery: bush, bush, and more bush – especially when it teemed with game. We suspected something dramatic when, on our way to Satara, we saw a herd of buffalo surrounding a male lion, which had been mortally wounded in a battle with a sable antelope. That was on the left side of the road. On the right side a rhino and a leopard had teamed up to fight an elephant, and the result was carnage, enthusiastically welcomed by four species of vulture, a family of hyenas, a pack of wild dogs, a marabou stork, and God knows how many dung beetles. And guess what we saw in the midst of it all? Yes: the rarest and positively the most beautiful (and dangerous) of the Big Five: a *Mitsubishi Pajero* with Bull Bars, electronically controlled sequential multi-port fuel injection, and a place to hold a can of coke.

Sick at Heart
[For those Zimbabweans murdered in the run-up to the delayed Presidential elections]

Late one morning I walked the night;
not only was the sky alight
with Scorpio, and fireflies,
and owls with disembodied eyes;
but scattered widely in the dust
a million diamonds keen as lust.

A million spiders' eyes reflect
my torchlight, and then I detect
ten million termites loading grass:
a mass oblation comes to pass:
upheavals of the motherland:
close the pits with shovels of sand.

Orion killed by Scorpio,
his dying light, his afterglow;
that tilting of the Southern Cross,
Eros spilling Thanatos;
bushfires dimming an errant moon,
the sennet wind a loud bassoon.

Late one morning, walking the night
like Dickens after Esther's plight,
a stranger, undirected, hurled
against an unforgiving world,
yet mindful of our mother's womb,
which doubles as a common tomb;

mindful too of shovelling sand
in rhythms of a saraband,
grand, triple time, long second beat,
laying to rest just so much meat.
Hear it clattering on the planks
of coffins – for this relief, much thanks.

Charles Dickens Visits Bulawayo

He dragged his foot like the devil,
he menstruated from his bum,
he was Sikes and Nancy: evil
and good: of opposites the sum.

He dreamed of being a singer,
an organ player in the church,
a quasi-corvid bell-ringer,
with a corvid's angular lurch.

Out of the wind, out of the grit,
in to the streets splashed with urine,
into the diarrhoeal shit,
sanctimony larded with sin.

My alter ego, John Jasper,
did he butcher his nephew, Ned?
Did I, God forgive me, murder
my sister-in-law in her bed?

In secret places mouldering,
her nightcap, camisoles, dresses;
I took this lock of hair, this ring,
from her corpse, but what distresses

me most, Jack, is that I died – my
last words – *on the ground*, before being
committed to it. Don't you die
like that! Shall we go sightseeing?

I showed him the nests of weavers
woven from wigs and extensions;
I showed him queues of school-leavers
with disappointed intentions.

I showed him rats like dalmations,
dalmations like insects of stick;
he said, of all my creations
Aunt Betsey Trotwood's the pick:

"Never be mean in anything,
never be false, never cruel..."
Captain Cuttle begins to sing,
Oliver begs for more gruel.

He dreamed of being an actor:
Every Man in His Humour;
I am Ellen's benefactor,
Bobadil, the rest is rumour,

Jack, rumour. You died on the job,
you old goat. You came in your brain,
clanging like the chain of Jacob
Marley, shuddering like a train.

I showed him the choking river,
the child with expressionless eyes;
I watched his white whiskers quiver,
his distant-winged white eyebrows rise.

Your knowledge of Bulawayo
is extensive and peculiar;
and now, dear friend, I must go...
it's all right to laugh but don't jeer...

my piles, all that blood, my sore leg,
the opium makes it much worse.
Let's part with a song, Lovely Peg,
stand by for the opening verse.

Who Will Guard the Guards?

Sed quis custodiet ipsos custodes? [but who will guard the guards themselves?] Juvenal had adultery in mind when he wrote that, but I use it in a Zimbabwean context where the distinction between those who administer the law and those who break it has become blurred.

Do not underestimate the guilt that runs through the veins of half-decent white people who, for decades, benefited by the exploitation of black and brown people. But don't take advantage of their guilt too often, like my erstwhile friend, Assistant Inspector Takesure Mararike [not his real name], who robbed me of my *Toshiba* laptop, my soul.

One morning I heard a banging at my gate, and there was Takesure with his pretty young wife, Cleopatra. He was a radio technician with the Zimbabwe Republic Police, and he had recently been transferred from Gwanda. He needed temporary accommodation, until the Force found him a house, and he'd heard that my worker's quarters were vacant. Indeed they were; for good reason. They consisted of one cramped room, a toilet without a seat, a shower without hot water, and a grimy fireplace. These *kias*, as they were called, symbolise the contempt with which settler employers treated their indigenous domestic workers.

I said I was ashamed of the place but if he was desperate he was welcome to stay there, free of charge for as long as necessary. That very afternoon he moved in, with his wife and three little children. I asked him to go easy on the water and electricity, both scarce and expensive commodities in Bulawayo, but he could help himself to as much firewood as he needed. (It was only after they had left that I discovered his wife had sold my entire woodpile to passers-by.)

The next day there was a knocking on my door and I ushered in Takesure, looking very smart in his police uniform. He told me, over a cup of tea, how tough things were these days of economic meltdown in Zimbabwe. He'd heard that telecommunication companies in New Zealand were keen to recruit radio technicians from African countries, and could I help him with enquiries. I sat him down next to my *Toshiba* laptop and together we surfed the internet until we found some friendly and helpful New Zealand websites. It looked as if there were indeed jobs going for radio technicians. I helped Takesure create a neat résumé, and we used my email address to apply for a job through Telecom Human Resources.

A week later, Takesure and his family were gone and so were my *Toshiba* laptop (my entire database), my son's bicycle, 25 litres of petrol, my backpack, my torch, and a change of clothes, which included my colourful woven belt from Guatemala, the only one in town. The local police would not touch the case, and passed me on to the C.I.D. who invited me for questioning the following day.

My immediate concern was to visit my internet server in order to download any emails that had accumulated since the theft. There was one from the Telecom Recruitment Team:

"Dear Takesure

A job opening matching your profile for a position of Help Kiwis get connected has just been posted in our Career Section. If you would like to apply..." etcetera. O the satire of circumstance!

The Chief Inspector, wearing dark glasses in a dimly lit room, was sitting at his typewriter when he motioned me inside. Laboriously he took down my statement shaking his head, as if in denial, at the mention of my chief suspect. He assured me that they would do everything they could to recover my property, and, when he stood up to shake my hand, I thought I saw my Guatemala belt around his waist.

The Cage

"This wire mesh is really glass," he told his child.
She looked at him with disbelief. "It is," he smiled.

"Feel it ... no, not like that, silly ... not with fingers.
Fingers are for touching, probing ... fingers pick, point,
accuse. Feel it with both hands pressed, as if in prayer –
one on either side of the mesh. Now, gently, move ...

She looked at him, his little girl, with bold surmise,
and something atavistic flickered in her eyes.

Sapphics to our Redeemer

Bless you always ever so jesus crispies;
bless you comrade violets, choklit-hitler,
daddy limpwrists, jesuitical chiefly –
M for mugwumpum.

Fisting father, babamku-roora, dhura;
ponda, hondo, toyota 4 by 4 by
fortune favours zezuru leaders, bleeders –
O for adenoids,

tonsils, dentures, mouldering corpses. Bless you
daddy long-lived, long-playing, long dong silver,
ruddy diamonds, platinum, iron whore, gold-
glinting incisors.

Thrusting speeches loved by the masses melting:
two ears for one ear and two eyes for one eye;
western traders hokoyo homos, no bum-
bandits permitted.

Pum-pamberi, land reform, love you uncle
pinch-cheeks, eyes like mulberries, pasi traitors,
masturbators, mapete! Bless you comrade
jongwe, s-saviour.

Two Metres of Drainage Pipe

My family say I shouldn't write about that time, it will just bring more trouble; but I am angry, very angry. When I saw Mrs Moyo's grandchildren playing in the discarded asbestos drainage pipe at the bottom of our property, I was reminded of my older brother, Lawrence, who died at Bhalagwe camp in 1984, a month after his eighteenth birthday.

We, my brother, his friend, Neva, and I were walking home from school when we came across a group of armed soldiers lounging in the shade of a marula tree. It was too late to hide so we greeted them politely and walked on by. I was about to breathe a sigh of relief when the familiar, heart stopping call came: *"Iwe!"* We turned to find them beckoning us with their AK-47s. We knew that they were members of the dreaded Fifth Brigade because they were wearing red berets and they could not speak a word of Ndebele. We understood enough Shona to follow their orders.

They drove us ahead like goats, calling us dissidents and sell-outs and God knows what else. When Lawrence tried to reason with them they beat him with the butts of their rifles. In all there were eight soldiers. They took us to an army base at an abandoned primary school more or less in the opposite direction of our village, which is in Bulilima-Mangwe District. Here we were loaded on to the back of a North Korean truck with about fifty other captives and taken to a camp just off the main road, near Antelope Mine. At the time we did not know it but this camp, Bhalagwe, was the most notorious detention centre in the whole of Matabeleland.

The women were separated from the men and I did not see my brother again until the terrible incident in the drainage pipe.

112   *Together*

I shared a 12 x 6 metre asbestos shed with 135 other women and girls. There were no blankets. There were no toilet facilities. We were crowded like maggots in the eye socket of a dead donkey. Before I was taken as a 'wife' by one of the camp commanders, my duties were to wash the soldiers' clothes and their cooking utensils, dig latrines, and prepare *isitshwala* for us detainees. It was dished up on dustbin lids with about 15 people per lid. We were allowed half a cup of water a day.

The ex-ZIPRAS had the worst of it. They were kept in a separate area with very low buildings, which had no windows, only ventilation slats. They were shackled all the time, and tortured much more than the rest of us. All day long graves were dug in the camp grounds, and when they were full, bodies were moved further afield and thrown into mine shafts. The screaming never stopped, and the stench of death never went away.

My parents taught us to stand up for what we believed in, for what we thought was right. Treat people the way you would expect them to treat you, my father always said, looking steadily at his son. Consequently Lawrence developed the courage of his convictions, a courage, which would do him no good at Bhalagwe camp. He was singled out as a trouble-maker and made to pay for it, and I was forced to watch.

A two-metre asbestos drainage pipe was rolled in from the Antelope road. My brother was forced to climb into the middle of it. Two other men, one of them Neva, were told to back into either end. It was a tight fit. The two on either end were then ordered to come out and as they emerged, head and hands first, they were beaten with heavy branches, so they scrambled, panicking, back into the pipe. Again they were ordered to come out, again they were beaten, and again they retreated kicking and screaming into the pipe. This pattern was repeated until my brother had been kicked and crushed to death. It went on for hours. Neva and the other man had to bury my brother in a shallow grave, which Lawrence had already dug. That's how the red berets and the CIOs relieved their boredom: thinking up creative ways of humiliating and hurting us, the girls especially.

"*Iwe!*" I shouted at Mrs Moyo's grandchildren, "get out of that pipe before I chase you out!"

Haiku with One Extra Syllable

All stories are true
Even those that didn't happen
Once upon a time

Rearranged Haiku

Governing in Africa
Is like sweeping leaves
On a windy day

Empties

Vusi sold grass brooms at the Hillside shopping centre. He was twelve years old and he should have been at school. He was employed by Mrs Ruchiva who bought the brooms and other grass products from peasants in the communal lands beyond the Matobo hills. These she sold in urban Bulawayo at a hundred thousand percent profit. She had to contend with inflation. To keep overheads down, Mrs Ruchiva employed so-called street kids. They were paid on commission: one percent of all the money they deposited into the crocodile skin handbag that emerged, open-jawed, from the tinted, electronically lowered window of Mrs Ruchiva's prowling *Mitsubishi Pajero*.

One evening, while Mrs Ruchiva's handbag was receiving Vusi's takings for the day, she spoke: "Vusi, you are my best seller. I need someone to deliver meat all over town. This job carries a regular wage, and I would like to offer it to you; but first, you must get a bicycle."

"I will try to get a bicycle, Madam."

"You have until the beginning of next month."

Vusi went back to his spot outside the Hillside *Kwikspar* dreaming about owning a bicycle.

He was about to 'close shop' for the night when a sleek black *Mercedes Benz* with government number plates turned into the shopping centre. It stopped right next to Vusi. Down slid the driver's window revealing a most distinguished looking gentleman with a shaven head and gold rimmed dark glasses. "Do you want a job, kid?" said the gentleman.

"Yes please, Sir."

"Are you a hard worker?"

"I am, Sir."

"Right. I've just purchased a property nearby, Lysander Avenue, and I have already found tenants who want to move in on Monday. My problem is that the garage is packed to the roof with rubbish. Can you get rid of it all over this weekend?"

"Yes, Sir." Vusi's heart was thumping. Perhaps he would earn enough to put down a deposit on a bicycle.

"Very well." He handed the boy two keys. "The large one is for the main gate, and the little one is for the garage. Can you find 43 Lysander Avenue?"

"Yes Sir."

"Good. I don't care what you do with the rubbish. Just get rid of it by Monday. I'll pay you in pula or rands once you've given me back the keys."

"Thank you, Sir."

The property was a block from Vusi's *kia*. He decided to start working immediately.

The previous occupier had been an elderly white man who had died of unrequited righteousness. He might have decided to live longer if he'd been aware of the value of the inflation-defying empties that had accumulated in his garage. All street kids knew the value of empties. They spent much of their waking lives searching for discarded beer or coke bottles.

Vusi couldn't believe his luck. Not only were there hundreds of empties in the garage but they were in crates, which made them a lot more valuable. All night long he carried crates to his *kia*, and all weekend he dug, with a borrowed shovel, a pit in a corner of the property where he buried the remaining contents of the garage, mainly cardboard boxes full of Rhodesian memorabilia.

By Monday the garage was spotless and the gentleman swopped his keys for 10 rand in small change. Over the next week, Vusi claimed the deposits on his empties at various outlets in town, and he made enough money to buy a *Raleigh Bomber* with two inch rims and a large metal carrier attached to his front handlebars. It would be perfect for meat deliveries.

Bhalagwe Blues

They kidnap these tourists, blame Zipra, blame me,
they kidnap these tourists, blame Zipra, blame me,
I say I am innocent, let me go free.

They laugh, call me dissident, spit in my face,
they laugh, call me dissident, spit in my face,
they force me to go to a terrible place.

We dig many graves every day in the sun,
we dig many graves every day in the sun,
they tease us then kill us, they do it for fun.

We cook for them sadza, we polish their boots,
we cook for them sadza, we polish their boots,
red beret, he laughs, then he shouts, then he shoots.

They tie rubber strips round my balls, and then beat,
they tie rubber strips round my balls, and then beat,
when they burst, cannot pray, cannot sleep, cannot eat.

Putting wires to my ears, to my mouth, to my back,
putting wires to my ears, to my mouth, to my back,
my body it jump like *umvundla*, then crack.

Pushed a cloth in my mouth, poured water, I choke,
pushed a cloth in my mouth, poured water, I choke,
they jumped on my tummy till everything broke.

They left me to die in the shade of a tree,
they left me to die in the shade of a tree,
they said, you can go, picannin, you are free.

Shards

In a low country clear of the hills,
near where the Shashani River spills
in a good season – discovered there,
Early Stone Age tools, hand-axes, rare
now that plunderers, from the Trekker
(known to his foes as *Ndaleka*),
through the likes of Carl Mauch, Thomas Baines,
to Cecil John Rhodes and other stains
of imperial ink, have come and gone,
some under the ground and some upon.

Rare too are the human bits that in
more recent times, still adorned with skin,
in that low country of thorns and spines,
just clear of the hills, long worked-out mines
like Antelope, there discovered,
dropped down abandoned shafts and covered
with leafy branches, clumps of grass, stones,
because the police have moved the bones,
some muscle still attached to a groin,
and a 1980 five cent coin.

Boys will be Boys

The scene was set for talks that would redeem Zimbabwe. The party in power renamed itself PAPA (Popular Association of Patriotic Ascendants), while the party in opposition renamed itself DADDY (Democratic Association of Do or Die Yeomen). A neutral venue had been chosen deep in the South African *platteland*, a holiday resort on a golf course designed by acolytes of Sol Kerzner to cater for the world's wealthiest tourists, who may be separated into four categories: sporting heroes, film stars, CEOs, and government ministers.

Zimbabwe was on the brink of civil war. The economy had collapsed, and with it the rule of law as well as the once admirable ethical system based on what Kenyans call *harambee*, where the welfare of the community at large takes precedence over solipsists who think that the world exists for their pleasure, a pleasure most frequently located in the belly and the loins.

These talks had to succeed. Both sides had to make compromises in order to establish some kind of power-sharing government that would draft a new constitution, a level playing field, as the politicians like to put it, so that future elections could be free and fair, as the politicians like to put it. A memorandum of understanding had been signed, a mediator from a neutral country had been appointed (an eminent person who dressed and behaved like the stereotype of an English gentleman, paradoxically, because he detested the English).

"Shall we begin?" purred the mediator puffing on a *Dunhill* pipe stuffed with *Three Nuns* tobacco. His silver grey Savile Row suit exuded a pleasant aroma of *English Leather*, which blended synaesthetically with the rich caramel of his *Chivas Regal* whisky, taken not neat, not on the rocks, not with soda, but with an equal measure of tap water. His choice of tipple set the tone, and all the delegates around the table were fondling glasses of the aforementioned scotch: doubles.

> PAPA: We as the party in power are 'concerned about the recent challenges that we have faced as a country and the multiple threats to the well-being of our people'.
> DADDY: We as a two-pronged opposition are in the process of 'dedicating ourselves to putting an end to the polarisation, divisions, conflict and intolerance that have characterised our country's politics'.
> PAPA: We are 'determined to build a society free of violence, fear, intimidation, hate ... er ... patronage, corruption, and founded on justice, fairness, openness, transparency, dignity and equality'.
> DADDY: We recognize the 'centrality and importance of African institutions in dealing with African problems, and agreeing to seek solutions to our differences, challenges and problems through dialogue under the auspices of the ... er ... SADC mediation, supported and endorsed by the African Union ...'
> PAPA: We are desirous of 'entering into a dialogue with a view to returning Zimbabwe to prosperity'.
> DADDY: And we recognize 'that such a dialogue requires agreement on procedures and processes that will guide the dialogue'.

"Good, that's very good," purred the mediator, taking a sip of his *Chivas Regal* and tamping the bowl of his pipe with a horny forefinger. Are you ready to sign?"

> PAPA: Not quite. It has come to our notice that our ... er ... colleagues from DADDY were given the table with the best view in the wine garden.
> DADDY: And it has come to *our* notice that our ... er ... colleagues from PAPA have minibars in their rooms, while we –
> PAPA: You have *en suite* bathrooms and –

DADDY: We never get a chance to use the spa because you –
PAPA: Well, what about those girls you were allowed to take into your rooms while we –
DADDY: Shutup!
PAPA: No, you shutup!

"Gentlemen, gentlemen," purred the mediator, striking a third match in the serene process of re-lighting his pipe, "let's have another scotch. Waiter! And while we're about it, let's find another venue, a five star resort where you will be guaranteed equal treatment. I know a place outside Jo'burg, which serves the finest champagne in the world. And the waitresses are topless."

DADDY: Bottomless too, I hope. Mine's a double.

There was much mirth at this joke, and as the glasses were re-charged – doubles nudged into trebles – PAPAS and DADDIES shook each others' hands and slapped each others' backs, and playfully punched each others' shoulders. After all, boys will be boys.

Via Dolorosa

"How far is it from Olive Mount
to the place they call
Golgotha?" asks the teenage girl
with a tennis ball-

sized foetus in her womb, rugby
ball-sized baby wrapped
in swaddling offcuts on her back;
vitality sapped

by stinking fistula, tetters,
itching warts, herpes . . .
"It's also known as Calvary."
Whenever she sees

a man she buckles like a card-
board box, and trembles.
They found her by the Trade Fair grounds
where the river spills

its horror on Bulawayo;
where broken bottles and plastic
bags, used condoms, faeces, mutate
into a spastic

objective correlative. "Skulls,"
she keeps muttering,
"the place of skulls; how much further?"
She begins to sing:

"How far is it from Olive Mount
to the place they call . . .
place they call . . ." then she goes silent,
and resumes her fall.

They flopped them on a wheelbarrow,
and trundled the three
along Via Dolorosa,
to eternity.

He Shakes More Than He Can Hold
[Wendell Berry]

Only the light leaves are stirring.
Your tea grows cold as you listen
to the generators whirring
like insects in the ears of mice.
Pale shadows on the leaves glisten
in recollection of her hair,
that time she dunked it in the sink,
patterned with dregs, darkening fair.
For hours you combed out the lice.

Now your tea is too cold to drink,
too cold for dunking petty cakes,
too cold for little children's sakes,
too cold for rectifying mistakes . . .
When you try to write, your hand shakes.

The Floating Straw Hat

The Mtshabezi River was dry but early morning lightning on the western horizon indicated that the first rains of the season were about to bring relief to the village of Isinga in Gwanda district. The state-induced food embargo had been in force long enough to reduce the entire village of 300 inhabitants to near starvation. They were surviving on famine food, which, in this arid region of Matabeleland, consisted of the pods of the monkey bread tree or *ihabahaba*. Their livestock, meagre at the best of times, had long since been consumed by vagrants, government officials, and the sinister Fifth Brigade with their red berets and AK-47s.

Commissioned in the first year of Independence, ostensibly to flush out army deserters known as dissidents, in reality to punish the Ndebele people, the Fifth Brigade were trained by North Korean instructors on the banks of a river that never ran dry: the Nyangombe. At their Passing Out Parade in December 1982, the Prime Minister urged the soldiers to "plough and reconstruct", a metaphor in harmony with his pet name for the Brigade: *Gukurahundi*, or "the first rain, which washes away the chaff."

Isinga's nearest neighbours, a few kilometres upriver, were rumoured to have acquired a consignment of mealie meal, sugar beans, and cooking oil from US Aid. Somehow, the truck must have dodged the numerous barricades that the police and the army had set up on all roads leading to and from Bulawayo. After a lengthy consultation under the *indaba* tree, the village elders decided to send fifteen-year-old Sandile to Ameva village to negotiate with the donors for a little food. There were no teenage boys to send since they had either fled or been killed. Not only was Sandile comparatively strong and healthy, but she spoke good English, and she looked charming in her new straw hat with the black velvet ribbon. It had been a gift from Aunty Soneni, her late father's sister, who had spent the previous Christmas with them.

Sandile was happy to perform this task because there was a girl, her best friend, in Ameva who attended the same school as Sandile, at Mtshabezi Mission. Indeed they were in the same class where they always sat next to each other and shared secrets. Now they would have a chance to braid each other's hair and catch up on local news. Sandile's grandmother, her only living relative in the village, warned her to keep away from men in uniform, and not to attempt to cross the river if it was in spate. Then she and a group of well-wishers waved the plucky girl on her way. One of the emaciated village dogs and a few little children accompanied her as far as the river crossing, and then she was on her own.

In the searing November heat, Sandile was grateful for her wide-brimmed straw hat. Occasionally she would stroke the plush of the black ribbon; it made her feel secure somehow. It matched the black polka dots on her white cotton dress, her only dress that wasn't school uniform; nothing, however, would match her orange *amanyathelo*, known as pata patas or slip-slops. A yellow-billed hornbill seemed to be escorting her along the narrow track, which followed the course of the river. She was fascinated by its clumsy flight, dipping and lifting like the soup ladle in the school kitchen. Storm clouds were building overhead. Was that a distant rumble of thunder?

Sandile's heart lifted when she heard the sound of singing coming from Ameva village. There was some sort of celebration going on. Surely the food truck must have arrived? She walked a little faster; she climbed an anthill and from that vantage point could make out one or two glinting vehicles around which the entire village, it seemed, had gathered. People were dancing, and the singing grew louder. Food at last! Sandile trotted and then ran the last 100 metres, taking care to avoid the vicious stud thorns that carpeted much of this barren earth. They would easily penetrate her flimsy sandals.

By the time she realised the vehicles were not supply trucks but Korean made armoured cars, it was too late. Three soldiers wielding heavy branches ran her down and proceeded to beat her all over her body. From her position on the ground, screaming and begging for mercy, she caught a glimpse of her straw hat gliding like a frisbee over the stunted mopane trees, on and on, till it disappeared over the river bank. The soldiers were cursing her in Shona, a language she did not understand. Eventually they dragged her to her feet and frog-marched her to the rally or *pungwe*.

The soldiers were lounging in the shade of a large pod mahogany while the villagers sat in the sun. The commander was a tall, strongly built man wearing dark glasses. He was about to address the gathering when Sandile was dumped in the terrified crowd. There was a pervading stench of offal and damp ash. "I am Commander Jesus," he told the crowd. His voice was deep and gravelly. One of the soldiers translated his Shona into Ndebele. "I am one of the leaders of the *Gukurahundi*. In my car there are some gallons of blood. Human blood. But my supply is running low. We are here to kill, not to play – to kill the Mandebele because they are dissidents." Sandile became aware of a hand on her hand. Painfully she turned to see her friend, Nothando, gazing at her with concern. She tried to smile.

"I arrive here to check up on my boys, and what do I find? Nothing. Beating up people instead of killing them. I don't mind if thousands of you vermin are killed or die of starvation. You ate eggs, after eggs, hens, after hens, goats, cattle. Now you shall eat cats, dogs, donkeys. Then you are going to eat your children. After that you shall eat your wives. Then the men will remain, and because dissidents have guns, they will kill the men and only dissidents will remain. That is when we will find the dissidents.

"Now sing, dance, wriggle like snakes in praise of Our Leader, who delivered you from the shackles of colonialism, racism, imperialism. Sing!"

The soldiers went into action with iron bars and heavy branches; and the villagers did indeed dance and wriggle and squirm; they did indeed sing and yell and scream. About twelve females ranging from little girls to ancient *gogos* and including Sandile and her friend, were forced to climb the tree that gave shade to the soldiers. Those who couldn't make it were beaten senseless; those who could were ordered to open their legs so that the soldiers could insult their private parts and ram sharp sticks into them. One by one they fell out of the tree like so much rotting fruit. Sandile may or may not have seen the sudden flash of lightning; she may or may not have heard the crack of thunder; she may or may not have felt the warm heavy drops of rain on her mutilated body.

Back in Isinga, the villagers waited excitedly on the river bank to watch the Mtshabezi coming down like a locomotive. They heard the roar, and then they saw it, a wall of water, shimmering like quicksilver. A cry of joy went up, and then silence, as Sandile's beribboned straw hat sped by.

English Sonnet in Broken Metre

When capitalism fails the rich
(it always fails the poor), a jism
reinvigorates the corporate bitch:
I call it bow-wow socialism.
Good ol' Uncle Sam, he saves the big banks
with tax-payers' money, tax-payers' sweat;
Wall Street billionaires, give him thanks
for winkling you fraudsters out of debt!
Dogknot socialism for plutocrats,
the broker-dealers' contingency plan;
ill-gotten gains made by ill-gotten brats
devilling themselves in the frying pan.
Where Bob's your uncle, the Reserve Bank feeds
cronyism, and the First Lady's needs.

The Honourable Minister Speaks
A Sestina

Yes, indeed, we have a culture of blame,
which we blame on colonialism;
we have sanctions, which we blame on the West;
we have floods and droughts, which we blame on rich
nations; we have sickness and poverty
and misery, which we blame on the white

settlers who purloined our land (bled us white!)
by farming it, mining it ... and we blame
them for writing poems on poverty
in Africa. Colonialism
has crippled our dear motherland, once rich
beyond riches: north to south, east to west,

you name it. But now, it has all gone west,
finished; our rites, traditions, have been white-
washed. "We gave you football," you say. That's rich!
"There's no accountability. You blame
corruption on colonialism.
Doesn't that indicate a poverty

of ideas?" No, my friend, Poverty,
inflicted on us by your men at West-
minster, reared by colonialism,
nurtured by imperialism, white
on black racism. "'Whatever you blame,'"
you quote, "'that you have done yourself.'" No rich

bitch *murungu* understands or cares. Rich
bitches like you, the queens of poverty,
consumers of black cock – you are to blame.
Like your Hollywood prototype, Mae West,
you want everything! Fuck off, back to White-
hall: patron of colonialism,

130   *Together*

protector of colonialism,
donator of crumbs, which fall from the rich
man's table. You sicken me, sipping your white
wine, snacking, eyeing my crotch. Poverty
in Africa sustains the greedy West.
J'accuse. You, your kith and kin, are to blame.

Yes, colonialism is to blame,
monstrous child of your rich, decadent West.
The crime of poverty is coloured white.

The Pact

Dorothy Noyes (no relation to the poet), who was chairing this evening's meeting of the "D--d Mob of Scribbling Women's" Club, took the opportunity of Harriet's slightly longer pause – about one millisecond longer, to begin proceedings: "That's amazing, Harriet! Now, Mavis, I believe you have a rhyme for us."

Mavis took a sip of tea to wash down Dorothy's banana bread crumbs, and unfolded her rhyme. It had been written in pencil. "Though I do find that banana bread gives me wind," said Harriet helping herself to another piece. "Sorry, Mavis, please go on."

"Talking of which," said Mavis, clearing her throat to read:

"In the crematorium,
Rising to the steeple,
Through the mouth and through the bum
Pop go the people!"

"Goodness me, that's a bit rude, Mavis," said Harriet with a mouthful of banana bread. "I wouldn't show it to Reverend Dhlamini!"

"I don't intend to. We agreed when we started this club not to share our efforts with anybody other than members."

"That's why we can write what we like," said Dorothy; "mine's just as bad."

"Go on, read it."

"It's in my head."

"Well, say it."

"Here goes:

Hi diddle diddle
She's big in the middle
From staring too long at the moon.
The puritan brought, (at the thought of the sport)
Up his food, in a dish, with a feather."

"'Feather' doesn't rhyme."
"It isn't meant to."
"But –"
"What about you, Jean?" interrupted Dorothy, "how is your play getting on? – your doggerel adaptation of 'The Elephant's Child'?"

"I think it's ready. I've got an excerpt to read – where the elephant's child meets the python snake."

"Let's have it," said Mavis.
"But why 'feather'?" Harriet persisted.
"Can't you see, it's an anticlimax, Harriet? You all expected me to say 'spoon'. Now, Jean..."

Jean cleared her throat and read:

NARRATOR: "It's the multi-coloured python snake
With eyes like the currants in a crumble cake
And a stare that would make a quaker quake,
And he says sarcastically:

PYTHON
SNAKE: Ssuch a ssapient little pachyderm,
Ssuch clever quesstionss make me ssquirm,
Which sspoilss my coilss.

ELEPHANT'S
CHILD: You must be a worm
Or an eel or a lizard or a length of rope
Or a tassel from the vesture of the blessed
        Pope...
No, you can't be a worm, you're much too tall,
Or a length of rope 'cos rope can't crawl,
Or a lizard or an eel or a tassel or a hose...

NARRATOR: And the elephant wiggles his stunted nose.

PYTHON
SNAKE: You ssaucy little malapert!
            Pressumptiouss, bumptiouss, ssnotty ssquirt!
            I'll teach you how to be polite . . .
NARRATOR: And he wraps him round and holds him tight
            And spanks the child with all his might
            Throughout the black and starry night."

They all sighed happily, four elderly women who had little reason to be happy. Dorothy spoke, pre-empting Harriet: "Thank you, Jean, it's delightful. Have you thought of expanding it into a full length play – using some of the other stories?"

"I have, actually. Perhaps it's something we can work on together. You can paint the backdrops and, with Mavis's talent, we can turn it into a musical."

"What about me," wailed Harriet, "all I can do is talk, talk, talk."

"You can produce the play at your school."

"Yes. Now, cheer up old girl," said Jean, "all is not lost. It's a good life if you don't sicken, and all of us, touch wood –" she rapped the table with her widow's ring – "are pretty healthy for our ages. And besides, how would we manage without your wondrous milk tarts?"

"I'll second that," said Dorothy, draining her cup of now lukewarm tea.

This restored Harriet to her natural good spirits, and she stood up to go and powder her nose. "Oh, but weren't we going to hear some of my limericks? Never mind . . . next time . . . and it's my turn to bake . . . this lovely new recipe to test on you . . . but I . . . ."

Jean, Mavis, and Harriet all lived with Dorothy in her large rambling house in Burnside. Dorothy's husband had died of lung cancer many years before, and four of her five children (and seven grandchildren) were in the Diaspora. Deborah, her youngest, remained in Bulawayo, interred at Athlone Cemetery. She had been killed in a road accident when an emergency taxi had knocked her off her bicycle. The foursome had, for years, been fellow congregants at the Hillside Church of Ascension, and as each became more and more alone in the world, with family and friends dying or leaving, they decided to move in together. Dorothy's house was the obvious choice because it was so large: five bedrooms, two bathrooms, lounge, dining room, vast kitchen with walk-in pantry, vaster verandah, and three fenced acres of vegetables and bush. They didn't have to tread on each other's toes. Their assorted pets were another story.

Mavis's old house on the outskirts of town, in Robert Mugabe Way, had become a shelter for elderly impoverished women, and was administered by the Anglican Church, with generous support from the Muslim community. It provided hot soup and bread, once a day, for the street kids of Bulawayo. Mavis's husband had taken his life when the total economic meltdown of 2008, Zimbabwe's *annus horribilis*, had ruined his stationery business. Her three children (and two grandchildren), like Dorothy's, were lost to her in the Diaspora. Harriet, a spinster, rented her suburban house to an emerging businesswoman who had turned it into a thriving 'home' school where Harriet was employed in a part time capacity. Harriet had taught history and English, and coached hockey and tennis for forty years before the Ministry of Education had retired her on a pension that barely sustained her pets: a one-eyed Siamese tom called Captain Hook, and a Maltese poodle with rheumy eyes called Tinker Bell. Nothing if not literary was Harriet Longfellow (no relation to the poet).

Jean and her husband had farmed cattle in Marula until, in 2002, a mob of angry squatters led by war veterans had overrun them, killing her husband and their pets in the process. The farm was subsequently taken over by a high ranking army officer. Jean fled to town with nothing but the clothes she was wearing, and was taken in by Dorothy. She had no children.

These old women had a pact: if ever life became too much of a burden for one of them, all four would die together, by sharing one of Harriet's milk tarts, laced with a deadly Chinese-made rat poison, readily available from street vendors, called 'One Step'.

They drove to Mavis's house in Dorothy's bright blue 1973 *Datsun 1200*, the boot loaded with garden produce to go into the soup. There was a bunch of carrots, some sticks of celery, a small cabbage, three green peppers, five onions, a dozen baby marrows, a birds' eye chilli, and two bay leaves. Mrs Jina had promised to bring a sack of potatoes with her regular bread delivery. Dorothy couldn't remember when last she'd had the car serviced, but it kept rattling along. At the Churchill Arms Hotel, with its mock-Tudor façade, they turned left onto the Matopos Road. There was a power cut so they would have to be careful at the traffic lights on Cecil Avenue. They decided to go via Hillside shopping centre in order to check their post box. It was empty. As the months and then the years went by, they heard less and less from friends and relatives. The children and grandchildren never wrote but there was always a hope, however faint. They did receive phone calls once or twice a year, and they did get an occasional little something from the Western Union; but memories of the recent past were blurring for these 'old girls' while the distant past – the good old days – came more and more brightly into focus.

Dorothy began to sing, and soon the others joined in:

In my sweet little Alice blue gown
When I first wandered down into town –
I was both proud and shy
As I felt every eye,
And in every shop window I'd primp passing by.

Then in manner of fashion I'd frown
And the world seemed to smile all around –
Till it wilted I wore it,
I'll always adore it,
My sweet little Alice blue gown.

Along Hillside Road to town they delighted in the heavily scented bauhinia blossoms, always at their best in August, the month when boisterous south-easterlies blew the winter away. The dumping of garbage wasn't so evident on these wider roads.

The entrance to Mavis's house was dominated by a magnificent *Aloe arborescens* now past its flowering prime. "I've been thinking and thinking about your jingle, Mavis . . . all those . . . here, let me help you with that . . ." they were unloading the boot ". . . my, what a delightful cabbage . . . oops, there's a worm . . . wormwood, wormwood . . . those references to breaking wind . . . you know, my pupils – "

"Come on girls," said Dorothy, "there's already a queue, and we haven't started chopping the vegetables." She headed for the kitchen with the others in her wake. The eight residents, all older than the man after whom their street had been renamed, already dressed for bed, greeted them in the wide passageway. The huge aluminium pot on the gas cooker would provide a meal for about thirty street kids and the eight residents. Any leftovers would be shared by Dorothy and her chums. A dozen homeless children had already gathered in the night-soil lane behind the house.

"I'll do the stock," said Harriet. She went to the fridge and took out a meaty shinbone, which she dipped in seasoned flour. "Where's the oil?"

"In the cupboard under your nose."

"There are still some potatoes from yesterday. Did anybody think to bring a peeler?"

"Look in that drawer." Mavis motioned with her chin because her hands were busy chopping celery.

"Matches?"

"Your face, my backside."

"That's not very nice, Jean!"

"Sorry. I couldn't resist it."

"Well, it's not very nice," muttered Harriet as she took a box of matches from Dorothy and proceeded to light the small gas ring. She put some cooking oil in the somewhat dented frying pan, added a chopped onion and the shin bone, and soon a very pleasant aroma wafted through the kitchen and down the passageway. The ancient *gogos* nodded their heads in approval. Harriet turned the soup meat over and let it brown for a few seconds before transferring it and the onions to the large pot, which was rapidly filling with a variety of chopped vegetables. Jean's insult, and the subsequent giggles, would at least keep her quiet for a minute or two.

Mrs Jina arrived with her two sons, lugging loaves of yesterday's bread, and a sack of potatoes. The donations came from her family supermarket. After greetings were exchanged, Mrs Jina informed the others that there was a small drama developing on the street outside the house. A friend of hers who was part of a constitution outreach team had come, at Mrs Jina's invitation, with a *bakkie* load of starving people from near Esigodini, to share the soup. "The problem is, they have been followed here by some very rough-looking youths. They were at the outreach meeting and they kept intimidating the locals, threatening to burn down their houses if anyone opposed a President for life."

"And I expect the police did nothing."

"They stood by, smiling."

"Look, Amina, why don't you ask your friend to bring his *bakkie* round the back, and we'll feed them too. The soup won't be ready for another half hour."

"'Amina Jina'," muttered Harriet to herself while stirring the soup with a large wooden spoon..."I like that."

Mrs Jina went back out with her sons, and didn't return; but she delivered the message to her outreach friend who manoeuvred his *bakkie* round the block and crawled in to the back lane, which was barely wide enough for a vehicle. The ZANU-PF youths, half a dozen of them, followed on foot, and waited – watching – in the shadows beyond the single paraffin lamp that illuminated Mavis's backyard.

"What are we going to do with them?" asked Jean, anxiously peering out of the kitchen window.

The soup was boiling merrily. Jean, Dorothy, and Mavis were moving piles of bread slices, enamel mugs, and spoons to the outside table behind which the children queued, twenty or so, patiently waiting. "We'll feed them," Dorothy called. "There's nothing like hot soup to create peace and goodwill among men."

Harriet wasn't so sure. "'Peace?'" she spat, "'I hate the word, as I hate hell, all Montagues, and thee'."

When the soup was ready, when the meat had sufficiently softened to fall from the bone, and the delicious marrow had dispersed among the vegetables, Harriet and Mavis, wearing oven gloves, lifted the pot off the stove and carried it to the table outside. First, a quantity of the soup was ladled into a smaller pot for the resident *gogos* who would eat inside. This was supervised by Jean. Next, the street kids were served. There was a zinc bath under the table half filled with warm soapy water where the mugs and spoons once used, would be deposited. Harriet was on washing up duty. Mavis ladled the soup while Dorothy handed it out, along with a thick slice of bread.

The trouble began when the rural folk were invited to join the queue. (Mrs Jina's friend had locked himself into his cab.) As they climbed painfully out of the *bakkie* – six skeletal women and men, the youths began to chant partisan jingles, similar to those recorded by the Mbare Chimurenga Choir and played every thirty minutes by the country's sole broadcaster. They advanced out of the shadows and it was then that the soup kitchen team noticed weapons: thick branches, iron bars, and knives. Dorothy appealed to them. "Please," she called out, "we are a charity. We don't engage in politics. You are welcome to share our soup."

"Your soup!" snarled one of the youths. "You whites are thieves. That soup comes from the land, which you stole from our people." He rushed at the table and overturned the huge pot. Its steaming contents fell on Mavis who let out a gasp and then fainted. While Dorothy and Harriet attended to their friend, all hell broke loose as the youths attacked the rural folk and any street kids who had made the mistake of hanging around. Mrs Jina's friend tried to drive away but his engine stalled, and while he was trying to re-start it, one of the youths smashed his cab window with a rock and proceeded to drag the outreach member, begging and screaming, on to the ground. There he was repeatedly kicked and beaten.

Jean bustled out to help the others carry Mavis into her house. (The *gogos* were cowering in their bedrooms.) They laid her gently on the lounge carpet; then Harriet rushed to lock them in. Mavis was semi-conscious, whimpering. Dorothy undid her sodden blouse and skirt. The burns were already blistering, from above her navel to below her crotch. Outside, the beatings had ceased and they heard the youths driving off in their government vehicle, a *Santana*, registered to the Zimbabwe Republican Police.

"Quick, all of you," said Jean, "get some aloe leaves, cut off the thorns, and then slice them through. Hurry!"

Gently Jean applied the cool, slimy poultice to the burns on Mavis's body. There was an instant easing of pain, the whimpering ceased. Dorothy found a towel in the linen cupboard, which she spread over the aloe leaves. "What shall we do?" said Harriet. They couldn't call a doctor or take her to the Mater Dei hospital because, like all of them, she was no longer on medical aid. The government hospital was an option but there you might wait hours in the queue before getting reluctant attention. "And what about those poor people outside? This is dreadful . . . my God!"

"Let's not panic," said Dorothy. "I know we shouldn't move her but I think she'll be better off in her bed at home than on this cold, hard floor. I wish we had some pain killers. All of you help me put her on the back seat of the *Datsun*. Jean, you come back with me. Harriet, you wait here until help arrives for those poor people outside. Stay locked indoors, and start making phone calls. Reverend Dhlamini will organize something. Now, let's move Mavis. Harriet and Jean, take her arms; I will take her legs." As they lifted her, she cried out in pain. Some of the aloe leaves slipped to the floor, followed by bits of carrot, celery, green pepper, cabbage, onion, baby marrow, and soup meat.

* * *

Mavis, looking deathly pale, was lying under a sheet on her bed in Dorothy's house. Dorothy was busy plumping her pillow, Harriet was trying, not very successfully, to feed her beef broth from a teaspoon, and Jean, at Mavis's gestured request, was reading her playlet, for children of all ages, about how the elephant got its trunk. Harriet kept interrupting the reading with desultory references to Dorothy's subversive use of 'feather' in her jingle, and to Mavis's scatological version of 'Pop goes the weasel'. "I mean, a rhyme is a rhyme . . . but you . . . just a little sip, Mavis . . . you . . . its shinbone . . . very nourishing . . . I didn't expect 'spoon', but 'prune', perhaps . . . here, let me wipe your chin. After all, the pip could do it, couldn't it?"

"Harriet, do you mind – I'm trying to read to Mavis."

"Sorry, Jeannie with the light brown hair. All is flux, nothing is stationary. Who said that?"

"I don't know who said it but I do know who sang it. John McCormack sang it."

"No, not that, the quote – All is flux . . . darling Mavis, would you know?" But Mavis was in too much pain to speak. "What about you, Dotty?"

Dorothy sighed. "I give up. Who said it?"

"Mavis knows. It's Heraclitus. It's a paradox."

"'Tell me what it is you eat? Is it bitter, sour or sweet? Do you treat it as a treat?'"

"'Much learning does not teach understanding'."

"'The elephant thinks and blinks through the chinks of his eyes in surprise . . .'." Jean was now picking lines at random. There was a note of panic in her voice.

They were all in a mild state of panic because Mavis's burns had become infected. Dorothy had tried without success to contact Mavis's relatives who seemed to have moved from England to Canada. Or was it Australia?

"I know," said Harriet, "let's have one of my limericks:

> There once was a donkey whose bray
> Was so loud that it blew out the day;
> A grateful old bat
> Circulated the hat,
> And they bought him a barrel of hay."

No one seemed to be listening. Jean had ceased to read from her doggerel play. "Well, how about this:

> A foolish Alsation of yore
> Thought his tail was the cat from next door;
> He could not explain
> A terrible pain
> When he ripped it to shreds in his jaw."

"Girls, we need to talk," said Dorothy, and she motioned them to the lounge. She coaxed them to a huddle, like a sports team before the whistle to commence play. They put their arms around each other, swapping scents of eau de cologne, lavender water, and *Johnson's baby powder*. "Mavis does not want to go on living. She's been in terrible pain for, how long now? Three weeks? And with the infection, it's getting worse." Harriet began to whimper. Jean was sniffing. "Now girls, this isn't the time to weaken; it's the time to be strong." She tightened her embrace. "Remember our pact? If ever life becomes too much of a burden for one of us, we go together. Remember?" Harriet nodded. Jean sighed. "Well, it's time. I can't bear to see that dear girl suffer any longer. Now, Harriet, make us a milk tart – and don't forget the special ingredient!"

Without a word, Harriet went into the kitchen while Dorothy and Jean returned to Mavis's bedside. Jean fetched the dying woman's brush from her dressing table and gently smoothed back her thinning grey hair, sodden with pain. Dorothy stroked her arm and hummed the tune of 'My Alice Blue Gown'.

The nutmeg aroma of Harriet's tart came wafting through to them and, presently, Harriet appeared with four side plates and four dessert spoons. Back she went to the kitchen, and returned with a dinner plate upon which the tart squatted, and a cake knife. She cut the tart into four slices, and offered them around. "Who's going to help Mavis?"

"I'll do it," said Jean Masefield (no relation to the poet); "altogether now, one, two three..." and because, as a consequence – she was the only one standing when they commenced their feast – Jean was the only one to confirm the manufacturer's boast that the rat poison, indeed, took only one step to kick in.

Yet Another Flower Poem

The American Dream is uncovered for being just that
in the flowers of the poinsettia, which are not flowers
at all but a series of scarlet bracts or modified leaves.
They recall the lips of Hollywood stars like Rita Hayworth,
and, most poignantly, of America's astounding poet,
Sylvia Plath. But this is my garden in Bulawayo!
What has the American Dream or "manifest destiny"
got to do with it? Everything, I guess; except our clichés
are different, like "Commonwealth of Nations", "rod of empire",
"Rule Britannia". And this shrub, *Euphorbia pulcherrima*,

adorning my early winter garden, concordant with that
afterglow of common thatching grass unsettling as its "flowers",
is as much a settler as I am; and the day that it leaves
is the day I leave: "For I have neither wit, nor words, nor worth",
as politicians have, and academics (a white poet
should restrict his content to the flora of Bulawayo),
"to stir men's (sic) blood". My settler friends and me, our destiny
is obscure. We measure out our lives in platitudes, clichés,
watching the sun set on Zimbabwe, as it set on empire:
scarlet and gold, heart-breaking, most beautiful – *pulcherrima*.

Emperor Moth

Order Lepidoptera. Among moths
you are a giant. You cross my threshold
late at night, gutter my candle with your
shadowy wings, chill my spine with fearsome
staring orange eyespots ringed in darkness.

Family Saturniidae. You seem
to sense my agitation. I recall
you as a larva gorging yourself on
bauhinia leaves; liquorice body
sprinkled with almond chips and candied peel.

Bunaea alcinoe, your feeding
frenzy is over; now it's mating time,
antennae combed for the occasion, wing
tips neatly trimmed. But you might burn your soul,
might lose, like me, your opportunity.

Such fancy names, night butterfly, for a
shriveller of leaves, douser of candles,
invader of these deliberate fools:
wingless but poised, nevertheless, pencil
and paper at hand, chocks away, for flight.

Bloody Diamonds

Abel Musundire might have been the child narrator in Emmanuel Ngara's celebrated poem on Nyadzonia, a Zimbabwean refugee camp in Mozambique that was wiped out by Rhodesian security forces at the height of the Second *Chimurenga*. Both his parents and his older sister had been killed, and it was only the shelter of his mother's body that had saved his life. From that moment on – he was just four years old – the thud-thudding of helicopter blades was branded on his soul.

After the war he had been reunited with his paternal relatives in Mutare. He grew up in the peace and relative prosperity of the eighties and early nineties. Following his A-levels at Mutare Boys High, he studied to be a school teacher at Hillside Teachers College in Bulawayo. After graduation he was posted to Gwanda High School where he met his future wife, Lindiwe, and where, when the Zimbabwean economy fell like a house of cards, he met the man who would lure him to a premature death.

This man was an inspector in the Gwanda Criminal Investigation Department, and a genuine war veteran with bitter memories of Nyadzonia and Chimoio, where he had been wounded in the hip. He walked with a limp, which he exploited in the manner of Long John Silver, to suggest aggressiveness. He was indeed quite a student of literature, and it was he who had introduced Abel to Ngara's poem by reciting it, one evening, on the verandah of the Gwanda Hotel. It was uncanny how the poem reawakened in Abel that terrible moment in 1976, the mangled remains of his family and many, many other refugees. He recalled with a shudder the rattle of choppers followed by bursts of machine gun fire. The inspector dictated the poem to him and he learned to declaim to his Commerce classes the opening stanzas:

We saw the soldiers come.
They came from the setting of the sun.
They came with armaments.
They came with fury.
They came painted like black people.

But soon we got to know,
Soon we got to know who they were,
Soon – the whole earth was athunder with bomb blasts,
Soon the whole earth was aflame with furious and
                                              frightening fire.

The fact that he had actually been present at the massacre impressed his pupils no end and they looked upon him with a new respect, not least the dreamy-eyed Lindiwe in his O-level class.

Abel was earning the equivalent of US$8 a month, supporting a wife and four children, when the inspector took him by the elbow and guided him to the Gwanda Hotel where he was treated to a fizzy drink – his first in two years. The inspector wanted to have a heart-to-heart talk with his friend. Had he heard of Marange? Abel thought he had. After all, it was home territory for Abel, not far from Mutare. Wasn't that where diamonds are scattered on the ground like flying-ant wings?

The inspector offered Abel a job on behalf of the wife of a cabinet minister, one of the most powerful men in the land, as a *makorokoza* or digger. The inspector was a *gweja* or dealer, who sold the diamonds in South Africa to connections in the ANC, friends of the minister's wife. The law wouldn't bother them because – isn't it? – they had the wife's protection. He dug in a pocket of his jacket and brought out a handful of milky pebbles. They made tiny musical clicks when he shook them under Abel's nose. There's a *Toyota Land Cruiser*, a plasma screen television, and enough left over to educate your children at the most expensive private schools in Harare. Abel moved to touch the diamonds but the inspector returned them to his pocket.

Abel was to work with two other diggers who had already been operating in the alluvial diamond fields in the Chiadzwa area of Marange District. They were quite close to the Mozambique border. Most of the poorer quality surface diamonds had long gone, so Abel was issued with a *mugwara* or iron bar to dig for the larger, more precious underground diamonds, which, processed, would find their way, eventually, to wherever rich bitches and their terminal husbands didn't pay taxes, and left their fortunes to Maltese poodles. Abel's fellow diggers were also school teachers, both from Harare. They warned Abel not to get his hopes up. They didn't get to keep the diamonds they found, and they weren't paid very much, but at least they could make ends meet. Abel wanted to have a word with the inspector who had promised him so much, but it was too late.

Too late – the saddest words in the world. De Beers, the original owners of the field, had allowed their claim to lapse, and it had been taken over by a British company called African Consolidated Resources. When it became clear, however, that there were rich pickings to be had, the government sent in the police to evict the foreign owners. That was in 2007. What followed was a free-for-all, a gift to the hungry peasants of Marange District from their ancestral spirits. A few of them actually got rich by Zimbabwean standards. But, bless them, the poor are not meant to get rich; they will have their reward in heaven. So in came the wheeler-dealers; then came the political heavyweights; then, and this is what spelled doom for the likes of Abel Musundire – then came the Joint Operations Command and Operation *Hakudzokwi* or No Return.

Abel's first night in Chiadzwa was his last. They were busy filling bags of diamond infested soil from their trench, when Abel's ears picked up a familiar sound – the rhythmic thud of a helicopter gunship belonging to the Air Force of Zimbabwe. He screamed to his companions to run but it was too late. Those diggers who were not mown down by machine gun fire were caught in an ambush of policemen and their vicious dogs. While the latter tore them to pieces, the former went through their pockets looking for stones and hard cash. Abel was lucky enough to be killed by the gunner in the helicopter, and he died with the sound of its blades thudding overhead.

Culture

"Culture is one of the two or three most complicated words in
the English language."   Raymond Williams

Culture is a patterned carpet, home to dust and mites
and unpleasant smells that linger.
Tom cat piss is the worst.

Culture gives you elbow rashes and itchy flea bites,
scratches from picked toe and finger-
nails. Carpets are cursed

with every stain and smear in the book of 'Handy Hints'.
Sometimes they enhance the patterns,
individualize,

like my old carpet, with its pets-and-children imprints;
threadbare, pocked with cooking-oil burns,
and rips like hornbill's cries.

When someone smugly says, "In our culture we do this!"
I recall a stink of carpets worse than Tom cat piss.

Waiting

I count the falling frangipani leaves.
Early April, the nights are growing cold;
the scent of wood smoke sours as neighbours burn
their household rubbish; every now and then
a discarded aerosol can explodes
triggering memories of another time,
another place, another war.

So quickly do they change from fluid green
to yellowish, to desiccated brown;
and yet, the drop, the clatter, ages takes;
takes ages: either way. In terminal
cymes some flowers remain, as white as wax,
mingling the bitter sweets of paradise
with odours of anxiety.

Like sharpening blades on steel the plovers cry
as homeless people wander near their nests
waiting for news, waiting for results. Who
will it be? These falling leaves remind me
that the day has come and gone for ballots
to be counted, results announced, and I'm
afraid that change will never come.

Glossary

aluta continua	the struggle continues
amandla abafazi	power to our wives
amandla amankazana	power to our girls
amandla isifazana	power to our womenfolk
amandla omama	power to our mothers
amanyathelo	sandals
amasi	sour milk
babamkuru	big daddy
bakkie	open truck
blair toilet	revolutionary long-drop toilet
chef	boss
chigaramakumucha	long earthen in-built bench in a kitchen hut
chimurenga	war of liberation
chirariro	the last meal before the burial of the deceased
doek	headscarf
dhura	expensive
freezit	frozen fruit drink
gogo	grandmother
gweja	dealer
handina	I have nothing
hapana chekumirira apa	nothing to wait for
hokoyo	beware
hondo	war
imi vemiromo mirefu	whistleblowers
indaba	meeting
inkosikazi	wife

inzwa	listen
isitshwala	mealie meal porridge
iwe!	you!
izintombi	young teenage girls
jit	highly danceable Zimbabwe music with fast guitar riffs and rapid-fire drumming
jongwe	rooster
kachasu	strong home-brewed liquor
kia	home
kombi	minibus
kongonya	raunchy dance style
kwasa-kwasa	erotic dancing
linjani	how are you
macomrades, maswera zvakanaka?	how was your day, comrades?
madzibaba	male members of an apostolic sect
makorokoza	gold and diamond panners
makuita seiko imi baba imi	what are you up to now
mapete	cockroaches
maputi	popcorn-like roasted maize kernels
matemba	kapenta fish
masikati vatezvara	good afternoon, my father-in-law
murambatsvina	'Remove the Filth': the destruction of homes and businesses by the Zimbabwe government
murungu	white person
ndatenda	thank you
ndokubatsirai nei macomrades?	how may I help you, comrades?
nharadada dzevanhu	sellouts
nyarara	keep quiet
padkos	road trip food
pamberi	forward with
pamberi nekunzwisisa	forward with understanding
pamberi nemi macomrades	forward with you, comrades
pamberi neZanu PF	forward with ZANU-PF

pasi	down with
pasi nenharadada	down with corrupt leaders
pasi nenhunzvatunzva	down with sellouts
picannin	child
povho yaramba, povho yaramba zvemadhisinyongoro	the people have refused and will not tolerate this nonsense (this is a song sung by the masses protesting against the decisions by leaders)
povo	the people
pungwe	all night meeting
roora	bride-price
sadza	thick porridge made from mealie-meal
sahwira	very close family friend who helps in times of crisis
salibonani abantumnyama	how are you, people
scud	plastic container for opaque beer, resembling a scud missile
shebeen	bar, traditionally serving opaque beer
shonongoro	tip, also money paid by relatives and friends of a husband to his newly married wife on the day of her arrival at her in-laws home.
shonongoro vatezvara	give me a tip, my father-in-law
siyana nebhaibheri rangu	leave my bible alone
siyaphila	we are fine
sungura	an offshoot of Zimbabwean rhumba and *jit*
taswera, chef	it was fine, chef
tatenda	thank you
tinokukwazisai vabereki	we greet you all, our parents
toyi-toyi	militant dancing
tsvimborume	bachelor past the age of marrying
umvundla	a hare
vabereki tine urombo	we are sorry

vakadhakwa	drunk
vapostori	members of a religious sect that blends Christianity and traditional African beliefs
vatete kwatonhora	aunt, it is cold
yebo	yes
yese yese ndinowedzera	give me any money, I will add it up
zambias	material used as a wrap by women
ZANU-PF	Zimbabwe African National Union – Patriotic Front
ZAPU	Zimbabwe African People's Union
zezuru	shona tribe
ZIPRA	armed wing of ZAPU

Lightning Source UK Ltd.
Milton Keynes UK
UKHW040037120522
402856UK00001B/93